A Woman's Guide to
Personality Development

Know Your Strengths & Weaknesses, and
Beccome a Perfect Woman...

Seema Gupta

Published by:

V&S PUBLISHERS
F-2/16, Ansari Road, Daryaganj, New Delhi-110002
☎ 011-23240026, 011-23240027 • *Fax:* 011-23240028
Email: info@vspublishers.com • *Website:* www.vspublishers.com

Regional Office : Hyderabad
5-1-707/1, Brij Bhawan (Beside Central Bank of India Lane)
Bank Street, Koti, Hyderabad - 500 095
☎ 040-24737290
E-mail: vspublishershyd@gmail.com

Branch Office : Mumbai
Godown # 34 at The Model Co-Operative Housing, Society Ltd.,
"Sahakar Niwas", Ground Floor, Next to Sobo Central, Mumbai - 400 034
☎ 022-23510736
E-mail vspublishersmum@gmail.com

Follow us on:

All books available at **www.vspublishers.com**

© **Copyright:** V&S PUBLISHERS
ISBN 978-93-813844-8-0
Edition 2015

This book was earlier printed in the name of *The Portrait of a Perfect Woman*

The Copyright of this book, as well as all matter contained herein (including illustrations) rests with the Publisher. No person shall copy the name of the book, its title design, matter and illustrations in any form and in any language, totally or partially or in any form. Anybody doing so shall face legal action and will be responsible for damages.

Printed at : Param Offseters Okhla New Delhi-110020

Dedicated to

*My Mother
The Late Mrs Savitri Goyal
An Epitome of Perfection
and
to all those who wish to explore
the World of Self-confidence and Perfection*

Acknowledgements

Thanks to my friend Rima Sehgal, a renowned psychologist, for her useful suggestions in compiling the Question and Answer sections.

To my husband, AK Gupta – for being my pillar of strength, throughout.

To my daughter, Aashima – for her undying faith and support. Her expertise in computer processing has also been of immense help.

Contents

Preface 7
I am a Woman 9
My Personality 13
I Wear My Attitude 17
Are You an Introvert or Extrovert? 21
Making Adjustments in Life 24
I am a Rational Person 27
My Trousseau 30
My Career 34
Fighting Stress 40
Cool that Anger 44
My Sensitivity 49
My Self-esteem 52
My Perception: Optimism/Pessimism 55
Am I a Loner? 58
Take it Easy 61
I Exude Warmth and Understanding 64
My Body Language 67
Psychological Growth and Self-actualisation 70
My Learning Experience 73

My Emotional Aptitude 77
Nagging Anxieties 81
God is My Guru 84
The Joy of Living 87
Weaving Dreams 90
I'm a Romantic 93
My Words Reveal My Inner Self 96
My Drawbacks and Guilt Quotient 99
My Charm, Poise and Grace 102
My Strengths, My Relationships 105
The Desire to Prove Myself 108
My Fears and Phobias 111
Perfection Personified 114
25 Tips for the Final Touches 120
The Portrait of a Perfect Woman 125

Preface

"She sings like the wind
She laughs like a river
She sleeps like a flower..."

When God created the Universe, He created Adam. When Adam felt lonely, God took one of Adam's ribs and turned it into Eve. God created both Adam and Eve with equal love and perfection. But Adam thought that since Eve had been created from one of his ribs, she was inferior to him in every way. What he did not realise was that he was a step behind Eve. While Eve was a perfect creation of God, it was Adam who was a rib away from perfection!

A woman is delicate and sensitive by nature. On the other hand, man is strong and impassive. There is no denying that physically a man is stronger than a woman and we all know that 'The mighty hold the reins' – which holds true even today. So in this man's world, a woman has to carve a niche for herself in every walk of life.

We talk of equality and women's liberation, but are we really there? To create a place for herself a woman has to slog and make many sacrifices. The poise and grace of a suave woman can take her places. She can be charming, endearing and sweetness personified. All she needs to do is develop all these positive qualities that are hidden beneath her shy demeanour.

This book is here to help you develop a charming personality, keeping in mind both traditional as well as modern values. After reading this book you should be able to slip into the role of today's Perfect Woman with ease.

This book will boost your confidence and turn you into a successful and Perfect Woman who is in perfect harmony with different phases of life.

This Perfect Woman fears nothing and enjoys everything in life through successes and achievements in all her endeavours.

■ ■ ■

I am a Woman

Am I a child or an adult
No, not one or the other now
One pace in front of childhood
And one behind an adult
Soon I shall stride into a new world
...The world of adult life.
—Margaret Lawrence

Being a woman is a beautiful feeling. A woman is God's most enchanting creation. Be it the paintings of the Ajanta and Ellora caves or the sculptures of the Konark and Khajuraho temples, Kalidas' Shakuntala in Abhigyan Shakuntalam or the Juliet of Shakespeare, the touch of a woman has turned them all into immortal creations.

Women are tender and their character can be portrayed vividly and beautifully in various artistic styles. This world is incomplete without a woman's touch. All creations of art appear dull and empty without the presence of female characters.

A woman's journey is a long one. From childhood to teenage to adulthood, a woman passes through so many phases in life with such ease and expertise that it is truly astonishing.

We have all grown with the times and acquired a personal self-image. Our self-image is made up of many self-perceptions acquired during our formative years of growth. The people who play a significant role in our lives and become our role models mostly influence this self-image. The opinions of our parents, peer group and near and dear ones help in formulating our aspirations, ideals and values. If their demands are unrealistic and increasingly cumbersome, we may tend to suffer from a low opinion of our self. But if and when we are unable to live up to our ideal self, or when our aspirations and others' expectations prove to be excessive or unrealistic, it is more appropriate for us to modify our ideal self as a way of furthering our self-esteem.

It is also necessary to check on your own level of growth. To check on your perceptions, answer the following questionnaire, which is an exercise to measure the balance between your self-image and your real self.

Scoring Procedure

Here are 10 items that represent your self-image. Make two separate columns, one for self-image and the other for an ideal image.

Write the score for the self-image (that is, what you actually are) in the Self-image column. Then answer this questionnaire once again and, in the Ideal Image column, write down what people expected of you. Consult the scoring key at the end of the questionnaire.

1. I am a self-centred person.
   a. Never
   b. Sometimes
   c. Always

2. I need to be assured. I have a strong need for approval time and again.
   a. Never
   b. Sometimes
   c. Always

3. I take life too easy.
   a. Never
   b. Sometimes
   c. Always

4. I am over-anxious. My anxiety hampers my growth.
   a. Never
   b. Sometimes
   c. Always
5. I consider myself superior to others.
   a. Never
   b. Sometimes
   c. Always
6. I don't mind being dishonest (like accepting and giving bribes). I believe in moving with the flow.
   a. Never
   b. Sometimes
   c. Always
7. I don't mind exploiting the female status to my advantage.
   a. Never
   b. Sometimes
   c. Always
8. I am tongue-tied in a group.
   a. Never
   b. Sometimes
   c. Always
9. I am over-ambitious.
   a. Never
   b. Sometimes
   c. Always
10. Everyone dislikes me because they feel I come on too strongly.
    a. Never
    b. Sometimes
    c. Always

Scoring Key

For every question you answered 'a', give yourself 5 points.
For every question you answered 'b', give yourself 2 points.
And for every 'c' answer, give yourself 0 points.

After you have awarded marks in both columns, add them up in each column separately. What you have before you is your real self-image and your ideal image. Now find out the difference between the sums of the two columns. This difference is the deciding factor as to how far you have been able to achieve what was expected of you in life.

Interpretation

Score in each column

Between 30 and 50 marks: An ideal score. You have great values in life. Although you may be an idealistic person, you have your feet firmly planted on the ground.

Between 10 and 30 marks: Your values in life are certainly different from the usual norms. But you are a practical person. And a practical person never loses any battle in life.

Between 0 and 10 marks: You are here for all the wrong reasons! You need to do a thorough overhaul of all the traits you have acquired over the years.

Score for the difference in both the columns' sums

Score – 30 and above: It indicates a low correspondence between your self-image and an ideal image. High ideals were expected of you, naturally. Unfortunately, you could not fulfil them. However, a high score difference in your real image and ideal image does not necessarily mean that you have problems. It only indicates that people around you need to be more realistic.

Score – below 30: It indicates a high correspondence balance between your self-image and ideal image. This indicates that you are living an idealistic life and have groomed yourself in ways that others appreciate. You have all the qualities of adjustment and will grow manifold in life.

■ ■ ■

My Personality

Sometimes you find yourself in tricky situations so different from everyday life. At such times, you are at a loss and cannot decide on what course of action to take. In such situations, your personality plays an important role in handling them.

Most of the time, our thoughts, actions and motives are governed by our subconscious. So we may not always be aware of the reason behind our own behaviour. But a reasonably secure conscious mind leads to a confident and emotionally secure personality. This security gives us a level of confidence and decisiveness that leads to a healthy and charming personality.

Take a bird's-eye view of your personality, your self-confidence, decisiveness and determination through the following questionnaire and gain an understanding of the hidden features of your behaviour and personality. To gauge your own level of confidence and sense of security, answer each question with either 'a' or 'b' and discover the hidden facts about your personality.

1. You go for an interview where you are interviewed by a panel of three members. The interview goes well and you are asked to join others for a Group Discussion in the conference room. You open the door of the conference room, only to find yourself facing a room full of young and smart people already seated beforehand. Do you:
    a. Develop cold feet and turn back.
    b. Enter the room with such confidence that it makes every head turn.

2. Although you love meeting people, today you are in a hurry. Just then you see an old friend coming towards you. Would you:
   a. Cross the street to avoid meeting her.
   b. Stop for a short while and tell her that you are in a hurry right now but will catch up with her soon.

3. Imagine a disastrous morning when your alarm did not go off, the telephone is not working, the gas cylinder is empty, the car ran out of fuel and there is an important meeting at your office within half an hour. Do you:
   a. Sit helplessly, head bowed in your hands.
   b. Face the situation boldly and look for ways to overcome it.

4. In the above situation, do you:
   a. Blame yourself for everything gone wrong.
   b. Give due credit to everyone concerned for the disaster.

5. In your office, do you:
   a. Follow existing rules with blind faith.
   b. Try making new rules that are convenient for everyone.

6. After graduation, your parents want you to prepare for the Civil Services whereas you are inclined towards the mass media and want to join a course in mass communication. Do you:
   a. Bow before your parents' wishes and forget your own ambitions.
   b. Make them understand your point of view.

7. You have gone out shopping. There are two dresses on display that you particularly like. One is red and the other is yellow. The salesman recommends the yellow one but your favourite colour being red, you prefer the red one. Would you:

a. Settle for the yellow dress just because you cannot say no to anyone.
   b. Buy the red dress because this is what you want.

8. Your parents have arranged a meeting with a boy for your elder sister. Both the families meet in a restaurant. Everyone is busy chatting when a protruding nail from a chair suddenly tears your skin badly. You start bleeding. Would you:
   a. Start howling and make a fuss, while everyone gathers around you.
   b. Quietly excuse yourself to procure a first aid box either in the restaurant or at a nearby chemist store.

9. Immediately after marriage your mother-in-law falls sick. While packing for the honeymoon you get to know of this. There is no one else to look after her. Your husband is also in a dilemma. Would you:
   a. Wait for your husband to give you further instructions on whether to pack or unpack.
   b. Take charge of the situation and postpone the honeymoon till your mother-in-law is well enough to look after herself.

10. Your child has suddenly developed high fever. Your husband is away on tour. You are new to the place, so you neither know the neighbours nor the doctors. Would you:
    a. Keep giving him a cold water bath and hope that your husband returns soon but not muster enough courage to take help from unknown neighbours.
    b. Go to the neighbours, explain your problem and seek their help.

Scoring Key

Assign 10 marks for every 'b' answer and 5 marks for every 'a' answer.

Interpretation

Scores between 50 and 100: You are open and confident. You seem to be sure of yourself and your actions. You also enjoy a high level of stimulation. You are a psychologically healthy individual who understands life and its complexities. You trust your own feelings and do not allow others to override them.

Scores between 0 and 50: You are mostly living your life on others' terms. Others dominate your decisions, which indicates low self-confidence and lack of decisiveness. You tend to accept their interference and decisions quite readily, perhaps because you wish to avoid confrontation. But shying away or letting them rule your life is not the solution. You must make others understand in clear terms that this is your life and you have every right to live it as per your own thoughts. To emerge from the overpowering shadow of others, ascertain the specific area of your excellence and devote yourself wholeheartedly to it. Success will not only boost your confidence and determination but also enhance your personality.

■ ■ ■

I Wear My Attitude

Attitude plays an important role in shaping many aspects of human psyche. It predicts and regulates human behaviour. The attitude you hold towards various situations affects your outlook towards life. Two individuals in the same place, at the same time, look up at the night sky. One sees darkness, while the other sees the stars. In essence, optimism and pessimism are products of our attitudes towards life.

Recognise your own thoughts and attitudes through the following questionnaire and gain an understanding of your views on life.

Tick the appropriate alternative from the following statements:

1. Do you believe in planning your tasks ahead and feel:
   a. Uneasy about last-minute changes.
   b. Try to adjust to the last-minute changes.

2. You are eagerly awaiting an important call when the phone rings. You pick up the phone only to discover that it is a wrong number. Do you:
   a. Get irritated, give the caller the choicest abuse and bang the receiver down.
   b. Tell the caller politely that it is a wrong number.

3. If you have to take any decision, do you:
   a. Depend on your gut feeling to decide.
   b. First analyse the situation thoroughly.

4. You are beginning a new venture that is yet to take off. Do you:
   a. Start dreaming with your head in the clouds.
   b. Follow a practical, down-to-earth approach and start planning.

5. You are in a job where you have to meet many people. In most official gatherings are you:
   a. The quiet type who stays in one corner till the end.
   b. Circulate amongst the gathering and make many new contacts.

6. You have been betrayed by someone very close to you. You feel cheated. Do you:
   a. Ridicule him by shouting and humiliating him in public.
   b. Take it gracefully in your stride with patience and stay indifferent.

7. You are getting late for office. While you are in the middle of your bath the doorbell rings repeatedly. Do you:
   a. Fret and fume in annoyance, but still manage to open the door.
   b. Ignore the bell till you finish your bath quickly.

8. The beautiful, colourful dress you purchased recently turns out to be a disappointment because the colour ran in its very first wash. Do you:
   a. Repent and give the dress to your maid.
   b. Take it back to the shopkeeper and firmly demand an exchange.

9. Your friend borrowed your favourite book but misplaced it and cannot find it now. Do you:
   a. Make her realise the folly through harsh speech.
   b. Remind yourself that it is only human to err.

10. An emergency arrives either at home or the workplace. Do you:

    a. Rant and rave and end up creating more trouble than before.
    b. Maintain your composure and solve the problem with a cool head.
11. When a salesman knocks at your door trying to sell some new product, you purchase it. Later, do you:
    a. Feel cheated.
    b. Remain satisfied with your choice.
12. Once again, it's your birthday. You wake up with the thought:
    a. Another year closer to my deathbed.
    b. A new me is born all over again.

Scoring Key

In your answers to the above questions, you respond with either 'a' or 'b'. If you checked 'b' 6–12 times your attitude towards life is strong and positive and you feel self-confident most of the time.

If you checked 'a' 6–12 times, it still denotes a strong characteristic but a negative attitude towards life. If your selections are scattered, read on:

Interpretation

A Type: Six or more 'a' responses denote you are cynical, distrustful and impatient. You tend to lose control easily and are inclined towards aggressive behaviour. You must control this dominant, possessive attitude that makes you outspoken and quick-tempered. Try to rationalise the situation and be more receptive about others' viewpoints.

B Type: If you have checked 6 or more 'b' responses, you exhibit a polite but firm attitude towards life. You do not get carried away easily and have a marked control over your emotions. You are considerate but do not allow anyone to take undue advantage of your kindness.

AB Type: The scattered selection of choices 'a' and 'b' is interesting. You are unpredictable. It reflects an attitude mixed with haughtiness, sensitivity and apathy under different situations. Your fluctuating attitude is the uniqueness of your behaviour pattern.

■ ■ ■

Are You an Introvert or Extrovert?

When we meet people, we respond in different ways. Some open up very quickly, whereas others take time. An extrovert is a person who is very friendly, open and ever ready to help, whereas an introvert comes across as a reserved, shy and quiet person who needs to be prodded for a response. Let's go through this questionnaire and ascertain whether we are introverts or extroverts:

1. When you meet people whom you have never met before, you:
   a. Make eye contact and begin a conversation.
   b. Talk to them politely only when they address you.
   c. Look elsewhere and reply only if spoken to.

2. When you attend a birthday party:
   a. You are the first one to greet the birthday girl.
   b. You wait for your turn to wish her.
   c. Sit in a corner and ask others to convey your wishes.

3. You prefer a job which involves:
   a. Meeting a lot of people.
   b. Public contact to a certain limit.
   c. Sitting in one place and doing your work quietly.

4. A match has been arranged by your parents; when the boy comes to see you, do you:
   a. Greet him with a smile and engage him in lively conversation.

b. Feel shy initially but soon overcome it and behave in normal fashion.
   c. Refuse to meet him alone. Take your sister or friend with you as an escort.
5. At your kitty party, you are:
   a. The most sought after member.
   b. Invited with the usual enthusiasm.
   c. Often the last person to be informed.
6. When you go shopping at the mall, you:
   a. Are warmly greeted by all the employees.
   b. Get smiles of recognition from some of them.
   c. Are not recognised by anyone even though you have been shopping there for a long time.
7. Your children's friends love to visit your house because they:
   a. Enjoy your company immensely.
   b. You provide them with delicious snacks.
   c. Know that you would be away at office.
8. Your status in your in-laws' house is:
   a. Supreme – no major decision is taken without consulting you.
   b. Moderate – you are consulted sometimes.
   c. Low – you are informed after the decision is taken.
9. When your birthday arrives, do you treat it as:
   a. A new beginning in life.
   b. Any other normal day.
   c. A year closer to death.
10. Behind your back, friends and relatives call you:
    a. Loud-mouth.
    b. Damn-care.
    c. Tongue-in-cheek.

Scoring Key

Assign 3 marks for every 'a' answer. Assign 2 marks for every 'b' answer. Assign 1 mark for every 'c' answer.

Interpretation

Score	Analysis	Personality	Corrective Measures
10–19	You are an introvert. This makes you a dreamy, soft-spoken and quiet person. But your aloof manner is mistaken for haughtiness. You want to get involved in activities but your basic nature does not allow you to do so. You lose many opportunities and might get secondary status due to your silent and withdrawn nature.	Introvert	Be bold. Do not let anyone take advantage of your shyness. Use your soft attitude to advantage. This world belongs to you as much as it belongs to outgoing people. So live life king-size.
20–30	You make everyone's lives more colourful. You are an open book with no hidden secrets. You immensely enjoy the company of people. You are the life of any party or function. People love your antics, but there are times when you go overboard and people wish you'd keep quiet.	Extrovert	By nature, you are pure at heart, so you are not afraid to speak your mind. This annoys many people. Try to be a little more diplomatic. Your open, outgoing and friendly attitude is a boon. But do not hurt anyone because of this. Check yourself well in time and remain in everyone's memory as an ever-smiling and jolly person.

■ ■ ■

Making Adjustments in Life

The secret of happiness lies in enjoying what one has.

Adjustments are part of our lives. We have to make adjustments in every walk of life. To lead a happy and content life, we must learn to be flexible and adjust to various situations in such a way that it ensures happiness for everyone.

Our level of expectations determines our level of adjustments and state of happiness. These two are related concepts. The better the level of adjustment the happier we are. Psychologists have discovered that people with better levels of adjustments tend to have high self-esteem, satisfying relationships and healthy physical and mental states.

Tick the following questionnaire to gauge your own level of adjustments by answering the following questions honestly:

1. Before going to bed, when you reminisce about the day's events, your thoughts turn to:
    a. The better part of the day.
    b. The mishaps you faced that day.
2. You relate to others with a:
    a. Positive attitude by paying them compliments.
    b. Negative attitude, picking out their mistakes.
3. Often, you trust others and later:
    a. Stick to your decision.
    b. Feel sceptical about them.
4. Jealousy, anger, contempt and revenge:
    a. Do not find a place in your vocabulary.
    b. Are an integral part of your personality.

5. Everyday while you pray to God, you:
   a. Thank Him for everything.
   b. Find it difficult to pray as you keep comparing yourself with more privileged people.

6. It's your first wedding anniversary. You have arranged a dinner party at home. Guests arrive on time and it is almost dinnertime when your husband calls and tells you that he has urgent work in office, so you may proceed and not to wait for him. You:
   a. Carry on with the party putting on a smiling face.
   b. Have a showdown with him on phone, then lock yourself in the bedroom, unable to face the guests.

7. You had a love marriage much against the wishes of his parents. When you arrive, you are not treated as a member of the family. Would you:
   a. Try and adjust, determined to win their love and affection with your sweet and adjusting nature.
   b. Coax your husband into setting up another house, as you feel suffocated there.

8. There are two simultaneous marriages in your family. One in your parents' house and another in your in-laws' house. They are close relations and you are supposed to attend both weddings, which unfortunately fall on the same date. Would you:
   a. Attend the wedding at your parents' place and let your hubby attend his family's function.
   b. Visit your parents' house for pre-wedding functions. And then attend the wedding at your in-laws' place for the full duration of the event.

9. At your workplace, because of the dominating nature of your boss, you are not at liberty to take your own decisions, so you would:
   a. Carry on till it does not disturb your self-esteem.
   b. Ignore the boss and do what you feel is correct.

10. When you hear the news of someone committing suicide, you:
   a. Feel sorry for her hasty action because nothing can be so bad as to give up one's precious life.
   b. Admire her guts.

Scoring Key

Give 2 marks for each 'a' answer and 1 mark for each 'b' answer.

Interpretation

Score: 0–6 (Need Adjustment)

You have a major adjustment problem. Self-devaluation, negative thoughts about the future and a pessimistic attitude play a dominant role in your behaviour pattern.

What You Need: You need better adjustment styles, an altered pattern of thoughts with high self-esteem, self-worth and confidence in your ability to tackle the situation.

Score: 7–12 (Trying to Adjust)

You are better adjusted. Conscious efforts towards making life better bear good results. But somewhere along the way you lose track and think, 'It wasn't my fault.' This hampers all further efforts from your side.

What You Need: Rebuild your self-esteem and sense of hope. This will increase your capacity to solve problems, making you a better-adjusted person.

Score: 13–20 (Well-adjusted)

You are pretty well-adjusted. You present the picture of a confident and self-assured person. You possess hidden leadership qualities and can rise to the occasion and tackle almost any kind of situation.

What You Need: Since your adaptability makes you delightful company, you should enhance this quality and maintain your well-adjusted personality as a role model for others.

■ ■ ■

I am a Rational Person

Attention, perception, beliefs and thoughts are the cognitive processes that affect our personality in a crucial manner. Our actions are often the result of our own interpretations and reactions to external events, rather than the events themselves. Many factors contribute to our success. Each one of us looks at them differently. This is unique and reflects our cognitive style. We tend to develop a world around us, giving way to our own actions and capabilities.

Individuals vary in their cognitive perceptions and notions, thus turning them into either rational or irrational persons. A belief in irrational ideas and assumptions often leads to self-defeating behaviour.

Find out how much you believe in the conditions that make you rational or irrational. Mark true or false.

No.	Characteristics	True	False
1.	You are well aware of your strengths and weaknesses.		
2.	You adapt easily to tricky and demanding situations keeping your pressure-tolerance quotient at an optimum level.		
3.	As a release from practical problems of living, you set aside some time for relaxation everyday.		

No.	Characteristics	True	False
4.	You prefer to live life as it comes. It also helps you shed minor irritations that plague you regularly.		
5.	You have little control over your mood when swept by emotions and it lingers over a considerable period of time.		
6.	To overcome an unpleasant situation, you think about it in a more positive light and reframe it.		
7.	Your optimistic views about life reflect your secure and healthy perceptions.		
8.	For you, life is horrible, terrible, catastrophic and awful when things do not go your way.		
9.	In case of failure, you attribute it to circumstances, not yourself.		
10.	Things may not happen the way you like. You may try to change the situation; if not possible, you accept it gracefully.		

Scoring Key

Add up all the 'True' answers, excluding 5 and 8, where you add the 'False' answers.

Interpretation

Score	Analysis	Rationality Quotient
6–10	You look at life with a practical eye. Your emotional status denotes vibrant qualities of self-awareness. You are well versed with mood management and self-motivation. You are sensitive towards life and show enough control through your rational behaviour.	High rationality quotient
0–5	You are impulsive. Your actions are ruled by emotions. Instead of rationalising a situation you prefer to get carried away with the tide. At times, it results in your losing out on the good things in life.	Low rationality quotient

■ ■ ■

My Trousseau

Clothes are one of the essentials of our lives. The choice of clothes not only reflects our mood but the choice of colours for the wardrobe can reveal our hidden traits.

Take these two questionnaires (A and B) that are specially designed to discover more about our inner self. Mark 'Yes' or 'No'.

Questionnaire A

No.	Characteristics	Yes	No
1.	Instead of always wearing traditional dresses, you have a collection of dresses of all kinds.		
2.	You always buy dresses on instinct without bothering about your pocket.		
3.	Your cupboard is full of dresses that you wore once or twice only, but emotional attachment to them does not let you dispose them of.		
4.	Others almost always appreciate your choice of clothes.		
5.	Your clothes are mostly in your favourite colour.		
6.	You always step out of the house fully dressed, looking prim and proper.		

No.	Characteristics	Yes	No
7.	The mention of a party always brings new clothes into your mind as the first thing.		
8.	The smell of freshly washed and ironed clothes is enough to boost your sagging spirits on a gloomy day.		

Interpretation

a. If all your answers are 'Yes', consider yourself a clothes buff. Even in your wildest dreams you wouldn't ever imagine being caught casually dressed. Dress to kill is your motto.

b. If your answers are a mix of 'Yes' and 'No', you consider clothes important but they do not hold the key to your life. You doll up for various occasions but are equally comfortable in casuals at an informal do.

c. If all your answers are 'No', you don't care about your way of dressing at all and do not put any effort in improving your dress sense either.

Questionnaire B

Our world is a healthy mix of colours. Each individual prefers certain colours to others. In their mysterious splendour, colours have a subtle way of signifying the type of personality you possess. Your choice of colour reflects your behaviour pattern. The colour of your dress, your wardrobe, your home and even your kitchen accessories is often an extension of your inner self, affecting your lifestyle.

Discover the subtle influence of colours on your psyche. Here is a list of 12 colours with their hidden qualities. Tick the colour(s) of your choice and discover why you choose that particular colour and how it affects your personality.

Red: The symbol of life, this electrifying colour denotes strength and vitality. People who choose red are strong-minded and have a materialistic outlook on life. Very warm and affectionate in nature, their generosity, love, courage, and even revenge are full of vigour, giving them a magnetic personality.

Yellow: Soul searching, astra-mental forces, mental concentration and the presence of intellect are the significant features of the golden shades of yellow. Bright golden yellow dispels fear, worry and nervousness. Yellow stimulates both the body and mind. On the whole, yellow denotes a soul that has spiritual qualities.

Green: Individualism, regeneration, and individual growth are the key factors of this colour. Green is the colour of success and prosperity. Successful and prosperous people invariably display a strong liking for green shades. Green also indicates independence and the beginning of a new life. Green has curative effects on the nerves and gives a refreshing boost to the tired soul.

Orange: A personality that is vital, energetic and active favours orange, which is also called the 'soul of energy'. These people frequently dominate others by the sheer force of their vital qualities. Orange expresses wisdom and reasoning power.

Blue: Inspiration – the spiritual colour. In China and Japan, blue is considered the colour of fortune. Its bright hue represents self-reliance and confidence, loyalty and sincerity. It also signifies an artistic, harmonious nature and spiritual understanding. People who prefer blue are loyal friends and sincere associates.

Violet: This is a mix of blue and red colours. Therefore, it contains the vitality and power of red and the spirituality of blue. It denotes true greatness, selfless love and wisdom combined with power and influence.

Pink: This mystic colour denotes a quiet, refined, modest person totally in contrast with positive, dogmatic and aggressive people. People who like a quiet life with an eye for beauty and artistic approach favour this colour. They evince great and lasting devotion.

Brown: This is a businessman's colour. It denotes brown earth ceaselessly striving to bring forth fruits of labour. No emotional feeling for this colour but it does depict great capacity for organisation and orderly management. Brown is the starting point of ambition and power.

Black: It is a negation of colour, associated with dark deeds. Devilry, hatred, discord and evil thoughts prevail with this colour. It is also known as the colour of mourning.

White: Just the opposite of black, it symbolises purity, openness, truthfulness, serenity, sensitivity, wisdom, refinement and spirituality. A constant attempt towards perfection and purity is denoted by this colour. Persons with righteous and truthful aspirations choose this colour.

Grey: The colour merges with people who love convention, formality and are self-centred. It denotes a lack of imagination and a tendency to narrow-mindedness.

Silver: These are jack-of-all-trades and masters of none. Persons choosing this colour are unpredictable personalities. Such people are versatile, active, gifted in various fields of life, and pursue all of them. Inconsistency, changing moods and feebleness predominates the silver colour. So be on your guard.

■ ■ ■

My Career

Each one of us is born with some inherent qualities. One of them is leadership. But not everyone can be a leader; most people tend to be followers. It is easier to recognise a leader amongst a group of people. Individually we all have a dominant set of motivations and needs that shape our personality and behaviour. So, in a way, we can say that we are all born leaders, the only difference being that some have these qualities predominantly, whereas in others it stays dormant or suppressed.

Would you like to assess your distinct personality that plays a dominant role as you work your way up, climbing the ladder of career success? Then answer the following queries:

1. Do you like to tackle situations that provide you ample opportunity to find solutions to the problem?
    a. I do.
    b. I have to.
    c. Why should I? It's not my problem!

2. You are offered a challenging job. Would you accept it, saying:
    a. I do.
    b. Do I have a choice?
    c. Why me?

3. Do you look for positions in which you are the ultimate authority?
    a. I do.
    b. I may try.
    c. Why should I? I am already overburdened.

4. Do you often enjoy reading/watching historical biographies of strong, successful and charismatic leaders?
   a. I do.
   b. I do not.
   c. Why should I? They are dead since long.

5. Constant comparisons are made between you and your colleagues at the workplace. Do you take it as healthy competition?
   a. I do.
   b. I try.
   c. Why should I? I have my own style of working.

6. When an opportunity knocks at your door, do you grab it without giving it a second thought?
   a. I do.
   b. I take time to ponder.
   c. Why should I? I am blissfully happy in my present position.

7. Do you co-operate and help others at your office expecting the same from them in return?
   a. I do.
   b. I do sometimes.
   c. Why should I? They are old enough to help themselves.

8. You have done a good job. Do you look for concrete feedback from colleagues on how well you have performed?
   a. I do.
   b. I don't mind.
   c. Why should I? I know my own capacity.

9. You love to make presentations at meetings so as to be the centre of attention.
   a. I do.
   b. I do not enjoy it, but I manage.
   c. Why should I? I hate probing eyes.

10. Your career is not of your choice. By a quirk of fate, you had to leave your favourite job, which you loved doing, and take up this present job. Do you still do your job with full devotion and give it your best shot:
a. I do.
b. I try to.
c. Why should I? I do not belong here.

Scoring Key

For every 'a' answer give yourself 2 marks. For every 'b' answer give yourself 1 mark. For every 'c' answer give yourself '0'.

Interpretation

Score 10–20 (The Achiever)

You are an achiever with the motto Climb every mountain. You are internally motivated and have high self-set standards and goals. Achievements are your major driving force. You can emerge winner in any situation with your hard work and cool-headed perceptions. You are certainly the leader of the pack.

Score 5–10 (The Follower)

You enjoy your work but you are not a leader. You may follow the leader but you do not take the initiative. When a path is shown to you, you follow it religiously. You have the capability but lack the zing that goes into the making of a leader. A little more initiative and the zeal to come first in every field can soon turn you into a leader.

Scores 0–5 (The Nonchalant Kind)

You have the I-couldn't-care-less attitude. You are nonchalant and indifferent towards many things in life. You prefer an easygoing life and do not believe in putting in too much effort into any task. You have the capability but lack the inclination. You can emerge a leader if you take more interest in your career.

Your Career Choices

Have you ever noticed how some persons are naturally much easier to get along with than others? Also, there are certain careers that are more suited to a particular personality type than the others. Everyone possesses a unique and predominant personality that provides one with different levels of aptitude for carrying out various tasks. These different aptitudes make you a good or a bad performer in your career, based on the balance between your choice of career and your aptitude for it. If you strike the right balance between these two it ensures job satisfaction. So enjoy a positive life by the wise selection of a job compatible with your aptitude and personality.

The following personality categories shall enable you to discover your best career choice.

Type A: Rachana prefers to stay aloof from others. She does her most productive thinking when she is alone in her office with the doors closed. She does not like meetings, especially the ones that involve many people. She thinks 10 times before speaking. She has lunch in her cabin and never goes to the lunchroom with others. She is the kind who would rather communicate through mails than talk a matter over personally.

Type B: Riya loves to be in the company of people. She does her best talking in meetings where she can share ideas with others. She never eats in her office. She finds lunchroom get-togethers and large meetings energising. Loneliness makes her sleepy and bored. She has the gift of the gab and an uncanny knack of convincing others.

Type C: Arati is the kind who prefers days that are tightly scheduled. She plans her moves, sticks to deadlines and is always sure of her judgements. She has a great sense of time and is never late for meetings. She goes with the tide and loves to be with people. If she ever came to a fork in the woods, she would take the road more travelled.

Type D: Neelam is fond of details. She believes in planning. She looks for practical possibilities in plans and proposals. She focuses on the current implications of an issue rather than the future ones. She prefers to think of herself as a pragmatist.

Type E: Sushmita has a natural tendency to take the road less travelled. She makes unplanned moves, permits herself enough time to work to perfection and allows deadlines to slip by. She has a general sense of time but is more often than not late.

Type F: Priya is a dreamer. She prefers an overview of things rather than the details. She describes things conceptually, overlooking detailed aspects. In decision-making, she looks essentially for future prospects rather than the current ones. She is totally devoted to her profession.

Scoring Key

Tick the category you think you belong to and then judge your choice of career.

Interpretation

Case A: Rachana

Personality: Introvert.

Compatible careers: Psychiatrist, Researcher, Programmer, Engineer.

Case B: Riya

Personality: Extrovert.

Compatible careers: Marketing Executive, Receptionist, Politician, Lawyer, Public Relations Executive.

Case C: Arati

Personality: Judging type.

Compatible careers: Judge, Physician, Manager, Civil Services Officer.

Case D: Neelam

Personality: Sensing type.

Compatible careers: Executive, Teacher, Banker, Businesswoman.

Case E: Sushmita

Personality: Perceiving type.

Compatible careers: Editor, Writer, Entertainer, Psychologist.

Case F: Priya

Personality: Intuitive type.

Compatible careers: Journalist, Philosopher, Artist, Social Worker.

■ ■ ■

Fighting Stress

In modern times, life moves at such a fast and harrowing pace that coping with it is not an easy job. Stress is the price we pay for being affluent and successful. But the fact of the matter is that events do not bring stress into our lives. Stress is the result of how we respond to these events. We all react to various situations differently, thereby experiencing stress at different levels. We can build up a greater tolerance for stress by changing our pace of life.

Answer the following questionnaire and discover your aptitude for stress management:

1. Your office hours are the peak rush hours for traffic in the city. To avoid the rush and reach office on time you:
   a. Leave home earlier than usual to avoid the traffic.
   b. Leave on time and drive haphazardly till you receive a traffic challan and a late mark on your attendance register.

2. Whenever you go out shopping with your spouse, you end up buying only half the things you intended to buy, simply because you cannot remember the rest. This leads to tension between the two of you. To avoid this:
   a. Do you always make a list of things and carry it in your handbag.
   b. Even if you make a list, more often than not you leave it on your dressing table.

3. You are aware that the best way to remember things is by noting them down. This also helps in attaining mental peace. Do you:
   a. Immediately note down things as and when you remember them.
   b. Often keep them mentally piled up till you jot them down on a piece of paper one fine day, once again missing out half of them because they have slipped out of your mind.
4. Whenever you are feeling low, your best drink is:
   a. A hot glass of milk or fresh fruit juice.
   b. A steaming cup of tea or coffee.
5. The last thought in your mind before you retire at night is:
   a. It was a good day and I managed to complete most of my commitments for the day.
   b. Oh God, I forgot to do this and that and this... (the list goes on).
6. Do you take your office work home?
   a. Sometimes.
   b. On a regular basis.
7. You have received a big and prestigious assignment; do you:
   a. Begin working on it immediately so that it can be completed within the stipulated time.
   b. Spend a lot of time brooding and thinking about how you can handle such a huge amount of work in so little time.
8. Work is important but sharing some time with the family is equally important. Do you often:
   a. Share some quality time and have at least one meal every day with your family.
   b. Come home so stressed and tired that even a simple question like 'how was your day?' evokes an explosive reaction from you.

9. You are a homemaker. You look after your home and family with love and affection. But your teenager, who was very obedient till now, has begun acting tough and giving you a hard time by exhibiting her independence. Do you:
   a. Realise that these changes are due to the growing phase in her life. You befriend her and try to be understanding.
   b. Give tit for tat with the attitude, "I am your mother. You better behave!" and enjoy the sparks flying.
10. To combat stress, a cool holiday away from hullabaloo of the daily life is your best bet. Do you:
    a. Often schedule some relaxation/outing for the weekend to break the cycle of stress.
    b. Feel holidaying is a waste of time. Weekends should be utilised for completing pending work.

Scoring Key

Assign 5 marks for every 'a' answer and 2 marks for every 'b' answer.

Interpretation

Score	Analysis	Stress Busters
Below 25	You are not dealing so effectively with every-day situations. This in turn creates anxiety and stress. You are unable to concentrate and get irritated very quickly. This also affects your efficiency at all levels and you lose many opportunities. Your physical and mental health suffers due to the continuous stress on your nerves.	You need a stress reliever like physical exercise, meditation, yoga, relaxation and a cool attitude towards life. Listening to good music also soothes frayed nerves.

Score	Analysis	Stress Busters
25 and above	You have the knack of managing stress successfully and enjoy better physical and mental equilibrium. You succeed in combating daily stressful situations by altering your lifestyle and modifying the environ-ment with a mature attitude. You are wise enough to handle a stressful situation as a challenge, turning it to your advantage for personal growth.	You are a cool person who takes life as it comes. A stress buster is not really needed but a little meditation, relaxation, exercise and soothing music can boost your stress fighting capacity.

■ ■ ■

Cool that Anger

The Bhagavad Gita says, "Those who are free from desires and anger and who have subdued their minds and realised themselves, around such austere beings lies the beatitude of God." Despite such noble teachings, we fall prey to a horrible malady called anger. Anger is a reaction to the situation that we feel is against our interests. We get angry for all sorts of reasons. Some of us remain angry for a long time while others cool off the very next moment. But the negative effects of anger remain the same on our mind and body, irrespective of the time period. So desist from anger.

Here is a quiz that will enable you to know the extent to which you can understand, manage and control your anger.

1. On your way to office, another car speeds up and overtakes your car from the wrong side, missing you by inches. You:
    a. Fret and fume, speed up, overtake him (in the process missing many other cars by inches) and get into a brawl with the person.
    b. Stop near a traffic policeman, complain to him about the incident and drive off.
    c. Cool yourself thinking that he might be in some emergency and put the incident behind you.
2. During your busy morning schedule a neighbour unexpectedly comes in and sits down for a lengthy chat. Would you:
    a. Tell her in a straightforward manner that this is no time to disturb others.

b. For the sake of courtesy leave everything and sit with her for some time, while fuming inwardly.
   c. Give her polite hints like keeping yourself busy with work while she keeps blabbering.
3. You are expecting a call from your husband who's on tour. Your daughter is talking to her friend on the phone, since an hour. After some time you:
   a. Can't control your temper any longer, disconnect the phone and scold her harshly.
   b. Leave the room in exasperation, fretting and fuming inwardly.
   c. Firmly ask her to disconnect, as you are expecting her father's call.
4. You are watching your favourite TV serial; suddenly the power goes off. Do you:
   a. Immediately call the electricity board, start cursing them and ask them to restore power immediately.
   b. Seething inwardly, sit before the TV screen, waiting for electricity to be restored.
   c. Stroll in your garden, enjoying the cool breeze.
5. Your husband forgot your anniversary. Would you:
   a. Get very angry and tell him how sorry you are to have him as a life-partner.
   b. Wait till midnight, hoping he might remember.
   c. Keep giving subtle hints. If nothing works, take the initiative and be the first one to wish the other.
6. Your boss has asked you to prepare a presentation. You are working day and night to complete it. When you are almost through, you hear that another person from a different section has also been assigned the same task. The two presentations will be compared and the better one will go for a final draft. Feeling cheated, you:
   a. Confront your boss and accuse him of giving you a raw deal.

- b. Instead of saying anything to the boss, you go to the other person preparing the same presentation and tick him off.
- c. Take it in your stride, thinking that competition will only help you work better.

7. You are travelling in a bus to office. It halts a long way off from your stop. Do you:
   a. Feel irritated and tell the conductor so.
   b. Try to rationalise and talk to fellow passengers about it.
   c. Take it in your stride and walk the distance.

8. Your child has not received good grades in her board exams and you are disappointed. Do you:
   a. Scream your head off at her.
   b. Show your displeasure by not talking to her.
   c. Tell her gently that although she has not done well this time, it is not the last exam. She can score better in the next exam if she works harder.

9. Your mother is old and bedridden. A maid stays with her the whole day when you are away at the office. But one day the maid does not turn up and you have a very important meeting that you cannot afford to miss. Would you:
   a. Take your frustration out on your mother, blaming her for putting you in such a situation.
   b. Be angry with the maid but keep quiet since she is not there and decide to teach her a lesson the next day.
   c. With a cool head try to solve this problem by finding other alternatives.

10. Your husband's boss has come over for dinner. While serving himself your five-year-old son spilled some curry on the table-mat and shirt. You will:
    a. Scold him for his manners and send him packing to his room.
    b. Give him a stern look and tell him to go inside and change.

c. Excuse yourself and your son. Send him to his room to change while you get the table cleaned.

Scoring Key

In all probability, in your answers to the above questions, you must have checked the same alphabet several times. If you have checked the same alphabet 8 to 10 times, your temperament definitely belongs to that type. If you checked up to 6 responses from the same alphabet, it still shows evidence of a strong characteristic.

If your selections are scattered, read the mixed temperament type.

Interpretation

Score	Type	Analysis	Remedy
For all 'a' answers, score 1 to 6 is indicative of Type A and score 7 to 10 indicates a definite personality type.	A: The angry young woman.	You have a temper and tend to lose control often. You also show a tendency towards violence. It may be an extension of a possessive and dominant personality, which makes you quick-tempered, cynical and impatient.	You must rationalise before taking any swift action. Also be more realistic towards others' faults. It's only human to err.
For all 'b' answers, score 1 to 6 is indicative of Type B and score 7 to 10 indicates a definite personality type.	B: impulsive yet sensitive.	You have a temper but also the ability to control it and have a marked control over emotions. Inside you may seethe with anger but outwardly you will not show it. This lends an image of a considerate, gentle person but an overdose of hiding anger may lead to a personality disaster.	Give vent to your anger sometimes in the same gentle manner that is your characteristic and do not bottle up feelings for too long.

Score	Type	Analysis	Remedy
For all 'c' answers, score 1 to 6 shows strong evidence of Type C and score 7 to 10 is indicative of a definite personality type.	C: Gentle and sensitive.	Your cool and relaxed attitude is just the opposite of the impulsive and temperamental attitude of Type A. Your gentle manner and understanding behaviour is much welcomed in this 'free to fry' environment. You are unaffected by calamities in life and have the capability to deal with them with a cool-headed attitude.	Everything is good about how you tackle anger, but there are chances you may be taken for granted and an over-considerate nature will be seen as a weakness. Analyse the situation and act accordingly.
Scattered selection of a, b, c.	ABC: Mix of angry, gentle and impulsive traits.	This scattered selection shows you are a mix of a haughty, sensitive, fair, impulsive and relaxed personality. You excite the adventurous kind because they can never be sure how you would react to a certain situation at any point of time. But stable and level-headed people may find this trait disturbing.	In life, stability is very important. There is a danger of this mixed personality trait tilting in the wrong direction, and all may not approve the dominant trait.

■ ■ ■

My Sensitivity

Sensitivity may be described as the innocence and spontaneity of the human soul. A mechanised and practical attitude towards life has robbed us of our natural sensitivity, which is the missing link between our physical presence and the spiritual self.

The following quiz streamlines our sensitivity profile, unfolding our self-awareness regarding sensitivity. Tick 'Yes' or 'No' for these statements. Don't give yourself time to ponder over possibilities – be as spontaneous as possible.

No.	Statement	Yes	No
1.	The last time you laughed was only a few moments ago.		
2.	The time spent with your loved ones is the most precious for you.		
3.	Your colleagues often consult you with their problems and seek your advice.		
4.	You love to dream and work towards fulfilling them.		
5.	After watching an emotional film you tend to empathise with the main character.		
6.	The smell of fresh flowers and chirping of birds is enough to raise your spirits.		

No.	Statement	Yes	No
7.	The smell of freshly wet earth from the first drops of rain is your best perfume.		
8.	You never forget loved ones' birthdays, anniversaries and other occasions. You always wish them with your heart, sending mementoes like flowers, gifts, cards etc.		
9.	Childhood images, memories, fights and then making up, make you feel nostalgic at times.		
10.	When your children fly a kite or sail a paper boat in rainwater, you join them with enthusiasm.		
11.	Life comes full circle for you when you spend time with your parents and your children together.		
12.	Your maid's child is your own daughter's age. She loves to study but cannot afford to. Would you help her out?		

Scoring Key

Assign 1 mark for each 'Yes' and no marks for each 'No' answer.

Interpretation

Score	Analysis	Sensitivity Profile
0–4	The music may be in the air but you must have the ear to recognise it. With the hectic pace of modern life and utilitarian ethics, your attitude towards life has become too	Need to cultivate sensitivity

Score	Analysis	Sensitivity Profile
	rigid. You have become what was expected of you, not what you wanted to be. You have buried your tender dreams into the dark alley. It's time you take them out to savour their beauty. Give them a prime position in your life, as they constitute the finer elements of life. They will transform you in no time and you will find the mystery of your real self unfolding before you like a flower's numerous petals opening one by one.	
5–8	You have opened the interconnecting doors between your emotional and practical life. You approach life with a subtle, confident and individualistic outlook. This has led to a quiet and serene attitude giving you well-deserved mental peace. This inner harmony reflects in your personal relationships, making you a very warm and approachable person.	Sensitive
9–12	You are in harmony with your inner self. You have explored the depths of your heart and are in close intimacy with your dreams as well as reality. You are warm, caring and sensitive towards others. This sensitivity gives you the power to excel in the fine arts. Intuition comes to you naturally. Knowledge and truth are your companions for life.	Highly sensitive

■ ■ ■

My Self-esteem

Self-esteem has a high correlation with self-acceptance. A higher level of self-acceptance helps us live life fully and be more accepting of others. Low self-esteem triggered by lower self-acceptance makes us rigid and more critical of others.

Answer this questionnaire to discover the level of self-esteem you enjoy.

1. My friends always say nice things about me. I feel they are:
   a. Genuinely fond of me.
   b. Exaggerating.
   c. Great actors and a bunch of liars.
2. My boss did not like the presentation I made with such great effort. He rebuked me at the staff meeting, so I:
   a. Apologised and offered to make amends.
   b. Was at a loss for words, trying to overcome the initial shock.
   c. Felt greatly offended and left the meeting in a huff.
3. I called my colleagues over for dinner. They want a drink before the dinner. I neither drink, nor serve liquor at home, so I:
   a. Tell them politely that they cannot booze here and give them other options like juice, cold drink etc.
   b. Show them the cupboard to convince them that I do not keep liquor at home and be apologetic.
   c. Send my servant to the market to buy some wine to please the guests.

4. My colleague and I were both recruited together. We received the first promotion simultaneously. Later on, she got a promotion before me and became my senior. I attribute this to:
   a. Her hard work and dedication.
   b. Her calculating moves to rise up the ladder.
   c. My lower capabilities give me an inferiority complex.

5. For my friends and visitors, I am a jolly person, ever smiling and caring, but at home I portray the image of:
   a. A loving wife and doting mother.
   b. A dutiful wife and harassed mother.
   c. A cranky, short-tempered and frowning woman.

6. While shopping at the supermarket, I meet many familiar people, so I:
   a. Greet them warmly and have a congenial conversation.
   b. Greet them if our eyes meet.
   c. Ignore the lot, because I am sure they do not like me either.

7. When I am at social gatherings, I dress and behave as:
   a. Myself, taking into consideration others' views.
   b. I feel appropriate.
   c. People expect me to.

8. I do not talk much in a group because:
   a. I am a quiet person by nature.
   b. Others do not give me a chance to speak.
   c. I fear I may say the wrong things.

9. When people think well of me, I feel:
   a. Good.
   b. They are exaggerating.
   c. Guilty for fooling them because if I were really myself they wouldn't think well of me.

10. Whatever I have accomplished in life is due to my:
    a. Hard work and dedication.
    b. Hard work and luck.
    c. Sheer stroke of good luck.

Scoring Key

Assign 1 mark for each 'a'. Assign 2 marks for each 'b'. Assign 3 marks for each 'c'.

Interpretation

Score	Analysis	Self-esteem
10–16	You are intelligent and clear about your goals. You are sure of yourself as well as the feelings of others towards you. You have the capability of adjusting to others and easily handle the upheavals of life. You have high self-esteem.	High self-esteem
17–23	When you compare the face value of people with their inner self, you feel dejected because many a times you find they are not as they seem outwardly. Still you are patient and flexible and deal with situations through a balanced approach.	Average self-esteem
24–30	Your sensitive nature and emotional upheavals make you see beyond the reality. This may be true, but at the same time it may also be false. You tend to go to extremes and overreact. This lack of bonding with people and no faith in yourself gives you low self-esteem, making it difficult for you to cope, concentrate and take decisions on your own.	Low self-esteem

❑ ❑ ❑

My Perception: Optimism/Pessimism

We all view life in different perspectives. A popular example is looking at a glass that is filled halfway with water. Some view it as a half-filled glass while others call it a half-empty glass. The first type are optimists who view life with a smile on their lips and the second type are pessimists who see only the darker side.

Questionnaire A

Let's check how well you know yourself with respect to perception, choices and views on life. Be honest as you answer the following queries:

1. You gave an interview in a multinational company. They promised to get back to you in a day or two. A week has elapsed. Would you:
   a. Give up hope and look for other job vacancies.
   b. Call them up to check the status.
2. You prepared exotic dishes, decorated the house and wore your Kanjivaram saree. You are all ready to receive your husband's boss and his wife who are coming for dinner. Do you:
   a. Feel something will go wrong.
   b. Sit down and relax.
3. During the above dinner some of your relatives drop in unannounced. You have no choice but to entertain them also. But your party is ruined. After everyone leaves, you tell your husband:

a. I told you something would go wrong.
  b. It wasn't as we expected but it wasn't too bad either.
4. Whenever you see a disabled person you:
  a. Feel depressed and think, 'It could be me'.
  b. Thank god for everything in life.
5. In a relationship, you are:
  a. Always afraid of it breaking up.
  b. Confident of a strong bond.

Questionnaire B

Here are a few words and alongside a pair of words describing them are also given. For each word choose the word of your choice from the pair. Don't stop to think. Be prompt and spontaneous.

		(A)	(B)
1.	Vacation	Fun	Expense
2.	Party	Enjoyment	Boredom
3.	Love	Bond	Bother
4.	Life	Beautiful	Monotonous
5.	Work	Worship	Drudgery
6.	Children	Nuisance	Lovable
7.	Morning dew	Wet fingers	Freshness
8.	Dawn	End of sweet dreams	New beginning
9.	Birthday	Lesser years	Extra experience
10.	Anniversary	Stuck for life	Sweet remembrance

Scoring Key

A. In 1 to 5 for every (b) answer assign yourself 1 mark each.

B. In 1 to 5 for every (a) answer assign yourself 1 mark each.

C. In 6 to 10 for every (b) answer assign yourself 1 mark each.

Interpretation

Score	Analysis	Type
0–7	You look at the darker side of life, which is why most things appear shady to you. If only you could learn to view things with an open mind your perception of life would change immensely and life will be much brighter.	Pessimist
8–15	You love life because you've learnt to enjoy its small blessings. Instead of brooding over things you take them in your stride. Your optimism can turn even the ugliest situation into a celebration. Keep it up!	Optimist

■ ■ ■

Am I a Loner?

Loneliness is a state of mind that reflects the absence of satisfying relationships. When we are introverted or have trouble in making friends or maintaining close friendship or relationships, we tend to drift away into a world of our own. This social isolation may be described as loneliness, which should not be confused with solitude. Solitude is when you are alone – without people around you. But loneliness is a state of mind in which you feel isolated, despite being surrounded by people.

Do you often feel lonely? To assess your level of loneliness and how it affects your lifestyle, answer the following queries:

No.	Characteristics	Yes	No
1.	Your parents were a working couple. Being an only child, you spent most of your childhood alone. Do you dread childhood memories?		
2.	Do you feel isolated, even when you go out with friends?		
3.	When people reach out to you, do you shrink back because you find their affection superficial?		
4.	Even though you have many friends, you feel no one knows the real you.		
5.	Do you feel that you laugh only to hide your misery?		

No.	Characteristics	Yes	No
6.	You are a sadist. Your miseries are your own creation.		
7.	A lonely evening at home does not bother you as much as partying in a group does.		
8.	When someone does not agree with your views, you feel left out and shrink back into your shell.		
9.	Your peer group and colleagues are nice and helpful people. Still in your hour of need, you prefer to solve your problems on your own.		
10.	You feel you have a lot in common with people around you, but you cannot share it with them.		

Scoring Key

Assign yourself 5 marks for each 'No' answer. Answer 'Yes' gets no marks.

Interpretation

Score	Analysis	Corrective Measures	Mindset
0–25	You are sensitive, emotional and vulnerable to loneliness. You are unsure of yourself and this leads to your not mixing with the peer group. Even though you get positive feedback from people, you refuse to accept it because you think you're unworthy.	You must work towards building your self-esteem so that you can accept life's virtues as they come. Also develop interpersonal skills to access people.	Lonesome

Score	Analysis	Corrective Measures	Mindset
26–50	You are well-adjusted in your peer group and social circle. You enjoy the company of others. Loneliness does not bother you because you have self-confidence. You are at peace and in harmony with yourself. You prefer direct communication with friends rather than bottling up your feelings.	Your well-adjusted, peaceful and harmonious personality is the cause of envy for others. Keep it up and spread your goodness around.	Well-adjusted

■ ■ ■

Take it Easy

In today's fast-paced world, it seems that instead of living life, we are rushing through it. Our daily activities are filled with urgency rather than the leisurely ways of yesteryears. We are on our toes, driven by urgency to finish a task in time, be it the ringing of the phone, answering the doorbell, a crying baby or getting children ready for school.

The overload forces us to tag the term 'urgent' with appropriate grading. And all of a sudden, we start living in different zones, finishing one chore after the other. This urgency controls and drains our lives.

Take it easy! Life is not going to run away! Time is still passing with the same speed; it is only we humans who have increased our pace. Slow down, take a deep breath and relax.

Answer the following queries leisurely and discover the pace of your life.

Questionnaire A

No.	Statement	Sometimes	Always
1.	I would rather pay extra than stand in queue.		
2.	Quality time kept only for my children is mostly utilised in solving other pressing matters.		
3.	I am grumpy, puffy-faced and tired when I wake up in the morning.		

No.	Statement	Sometimes	Always
4.	When someone is talking to me, my mind is often occupied elsewhere.		
5.	I keep postponing my recreation/ hobbies/favourite book to a day that is yet to come.		

Questionnaire B: From the statements below mark your irritants and joys.

You feel more miserable, when you:
1. (a) Misplace a valuable thing.
   (b) Miss the bus to office.
2. (a) Face indifferent neighbours.
   (b) Encounter friendly neighbours who love to drop in unannounced for lengthy chats.
3. (a) Do not have a fat bank balance.
   (b) Do not have a secure job.
4. (a) Have people coming to fulfil social obligations.
   (b) Have to go to fulfil social obligations.
5. (a) Are late returning home from office.
   (b) Are late leaving for office.

You feel good when you:
1. (a) Get free time to relax.
   (b) Get more work.
2. (a) Find your children fit.
   (b) Find yourself fit.
3. (a) Cooked a healthy and wholesome meal.
   (b) Prepared a ready-to-eat meal in a jiffy.
4. (a) Wake up late but well rested.
   (b) Wake up on time, but still feel sleepy.

5. (a) Witness big drops of rain falling even though they may delay your daily routine.
   (b) See a clear sunny sky even in the hot month of May because it will not hamper your activities.

Scoring Key

For Questionnaire A Always = 2 marks. Sometimes = 1 mark. For Questionnaire B assign 2 marks for each 'b' answer. Assign 1 mark for each 'a' answer.

Interpretation

Score	Analysis	Lifestyles
0–15	You know the difference between rushing through things and giving priority to things. You are balanced enough to deal with important jobs first rather than trying to do everything at the same time. Division of jobs gives you ample time to prepare for the next job. This helps you in acquiring a relaxed, flexible and spontaneous attitude. Your confidence and level of dedication is everyone's envy. Instead of wasting time, you utilise it in acquiring wisdom.	Easygoing
16–30	You are always on the move. Urgency controls your life. You have a list of important things at the back of your mind but you find lack of time a plausible excuse for pushing them in the background. Urgency gives you a high and you feel exhilarated by exhibiting how busy you always are. What you must realise is that this is destructive behaviour that devours all your energy, leaving you devoid of warmth and love in relationships. Shake it off before you become its slave. Learn to relax and develop interpersonal relationships. Soon you will find yourself enjoying life.	Urgency addict

■ ■ ■

I Exude Warmth and Understanding

She springs like a beam on the brow of a tide
She falls like a tear from the eyes of a bride
—Sarojini Naidu

Empathy is the identification of one's self with that of another. Our empathetic persona helps us be sensitive to others and their emotions. Empathy increases the power of a person as a perceiver and a communicator. It also helps us correctly estimate the general reaction of our peer group. The tendency to assume similarities between oneself and others is a natural phenomenon.

Tick the answer you consider correct.

1. If you want something, be it in a relationship, job or life, do you:
   a. Seek it at all cost.
   b. Go for it, but not by causing pain to others.

2. You are interested in knowing about your friends' life and career:
   a. So that you can do far better than them.
   b. For their well-being and growth.

3. While watching an emotional serial, you are easily moved to:
   a. Laughter, because you find it all make-believe and amusing.
   b. Tears, because you empathise with the character.

4. Temperamentally you view your relationships as a:
   a. Sceptic.
   b. Believer.
5. 'Think before you speak' is a saying, you:
   a. Do not believe in.
   b. Firmly believe in.
6. You are comfortable in company. When you are alone:
   a. You feel restless.
   b. You wish you had company, but at times you enjoy your solitude too.
7. You do not hesitate in correcting people because:
   a. They may not be wrong but they irritate you.
   b. They were wrong and you do not want them to repeat the mistake.
8. While travelling in a bus to your home, the thought of your family and friends brings:
   a. The tension of having to deal with them.
   b. A smile on your lips.
9. A beggar woman with a newborn is standing near your car window. Do you:
   a. Turn your face away, calling her a crook.
   b. Feel sorry for her and try to help out.
10. As per the custom in your family, intercaste marriages are not allowed. If your son wanted to marry a girl from another caste, would you:
    a. Sternly oppose him to the extent of disowning him.
    b. Allow him to marry her for the sake of his happiness.

Scoring Key

Give yourself 1 mark for all 'a' answers. Give yourself 2 marks for all 'b' answers.

Interpretation

Score	Analysis	Improvement
0–12	You approach life with a self-centred attitude. Your lukewarm reaction to others' empathies drives you to a tendency towards selfishness. You mistrust others and value your own plans, ambitions and views above anything else. People fear you and do not love you.	You need to sensitise yourself to develop a welcome and pleasing personality.
13–20	You are an empathetic person exhibiting a warm and understanding personality. You lend a sympathetic ear and a helping hand, not only to your peer group, but also to the outside world, generously. Your humanitarian nature makes you an invaluable friend. Your compassion is the secret of your dependable personality.	Although you have a great empathetic persona, there may be times when people take advantage of your sensitive and helpful nature. So before you rise to the occasion, assess your acts rationally so that no one can take undue advantage of your goodness.

■ ■ ■

My Body Language

Most often words are used for communication. But there are times when words fail in this regard. In such situations, a subtle gesture speaks volumes. Gestures reveal the person's nature and attitude without the use of words. Gestures are like words in body language indicating whether a person is friendly, defensive, truthful, lying, anxious or bored. A good reader of body language can quickly decipher these signs. These gesticulations are the result of our subconscious taking over.

Try and read others as well as your own gestures and think about the emotional spectrum they portray:

A. When you sit, do you often:
  1. Sit straddling a chair (chair's back in front serving as a shield).
  2. Sit with your arms crossed.
  3. Fidget in the chair, as if bugs are biting you.
  4. Sit on the edge giving the impression that you are about to run away.
  5. Grip the arms of the chair.
  6. Lock your ankles behind your legs under the chair.

B. When you walk, you habitually:
  1. Walk faster, leaving the arms free to swing.
  2. Walk slowly with hands in the pocket.
  3. Keep your hands locked behind the back.
  4. Keep your eyes to the ground and never look up.

C. When you talk, do you:
1. Avoid eye contact with the person you are talking to.
2. Look straight into the eyes of the other person while proving your point.
3. Shrug your shoulders often.
4. Keep your hands open while emphasising your point.
5. Keep clearing your throat before beginning a sentence.
6. Include verbal ticks like 'you see', 'you know' etc too often in the conversation.

D. Your smile reveals the most as you flash it. Do you often:
1. Give a half-smile.
2. Give a smile keeping your teeth unexposed.
3. Give a toothy smile.
4. Rarely smile.

E. When you are taken to task by your parents/boss/elders, you often:
1. Do not make any eye contact.
2. Clasp and wring your hands while talking.
3. Look down.
4. Wet your lips.
5. Rub your nose.
6. Scratch your head/smooth your hair.
7. Rub the forehead/neck.

Scoring Key and Interpretation

A 'Yes' answer to each gesture denotes the following personality traits that your body language depicts.

Group	Gestures	Personality Traits
A.	1.	Aggressive.
	2.	Rigid, crystallised attitude, fixed thinking.
	3.	Bored, unstimulated, uncomfortable.
	4.	Tense, withdrawn attitude, edgy.
	5.	Stressed, apprehensive.
	6.	Dissatisfied with conversation, tense.
B.	1.	Goal seeking, highly motivated.
	2.	Suspicious and secretive.
	3.	Slow-paced approach to life.
	4.	Never too sure of yourself.
C.	1.	Shy, introverted, secretive.
	2.	Confident, extrovert.
	3.	Sincerity, truthfulness.
	4.	Openness, honesty.
	5.	Uncertainty. Apprehensive approach.
	6.	Abstract thinking.
D.	1.	Subtle, coy and humorous.
	2.	Simple smile, reserved nature.
	3.	Warm and friendly.
	4.	Rigid and unfriendly manner.
E.	1.	Lying, fear of being caught.
	2.	Apprehension of tackling charges against oneself.
	3.	Attempt to hide your latent feelings.
	4.	Nervousness.
	5.	Impatience.
	6.	Gaining more time to think of excuses.
	7.	Trying to cover up something.

■■■

Psychological Growth and Self-actualisation

The two terms, psychological growth and self-actualisation, are so inextricably linked that there is a very thin line of demarcation between them. Psychological growth is when you have attained a certain level of functioning overcoming any resistance to growth. This comes to you naturally if you have an intense desire to grow. Self-actualisation is when you have reached an optimal level of growth that is more than the average person. Such self-actualised persons have a much healthier outlook towards life and they can put their talents and strengths to the best possible use.

An appreciation of everyday realities, a fresh view of life, greater acceptance of themselves and others, higher creativity and great resistance to conformity are all indicative of a self-actualised person.

To assess your own level of psychological growth and self-actualisation take this quick questionnaire:

1. You are going to the US for training. You would be away for almost six months. Your parents are there at the airport to see you off. At the time of departure, do you:
   a. Hold back your tears and turn away.
   b. Hug you parents and let them know your feelings.
2. During the summer holidays, you invite friends over to your house for a party. They all turn down your offer on some pretext or the other. Do you:

a. Feel dejected.
   b. Look for other ways to keep yourself occupied.
3. A friend approaches you for advice on a particular topic. Do you:
   a. Feel good and readily oblige.
   b. Oblige her feeling you are God's gift to this world.
4. When you are feeling down, you turn to:
   a. Your pillow.
   b. Your hobby.
5. You are offered a project by your boss that you are well aware is time-consuming and challenging, but its completion offers you good prospects. Would you:
   a. Accept the challenge and work on it wholeheartedly.
   b. Refuse to take it up, thinking it is too much work.
6. Everyday you leave for work in the morning feeling on top of the world. After a few hours in the office, you are down with 'Nobody gives me my due' syndrome. These shifts in your mindset are:
   a. Quite frequent.
   b. Rare and short-lived.
7. You overhear your best friend telling another common friend that she finds your dress sense atrocious. You are hurt. Would you:
   a. Speak to her and find out the real reason so that you can rectify shortcomings.
   b. Stop talking to your friend.
8. Despite your best efforts, you could not secure the excellent job you were aiming for. Instead, your friend – who is far less talented than you – managed to get it. Do you:
   a. Ignore her the next time you meet her.
   b. Congratulate her on her success.
9. One fine day as you go shopping, you find your boyfriend with your best friend at the ice-cream parlour

enjoying themselves immensely. You are burning with jealousy and anger. Would you:
   a. Face them there and then and demand an explanation.
   b. Act normal and wait for the right moment to query them.
10. After marriage, you realise that your husband is very fond of good food and your mother-in-law is an excellent cook. Your cooking skills are no patch on hers. Would you:
   a. Help her in the kitchen and learn as much as you can.
   b. Back out and leave the kitchen and cooking to her while you sit back and enjoy.

Scoring Key

1. a-1, b-2   2. a-1, b-2
3. a-2, b-1   4. a-1, b-2
5. a-2, b-1   6. a-1, b-2
7. a-2, b-1   8. a-1, b-2
9. a-1, b-2   10. a-2, b-1

Interpretation

Score	Analysis
0–10	You are yet to create a balance between your level of motivation and self-esteem. You are introverted, impressionable, and vulnerable to the ways of this wicked world. You must develop your self-esteem by being more strong, bold and realistic.
11–20	You believe in yourself. You have strong will power and faith in your abilities. Negative thoughts do not enter your mind. Your sound psychological growth and high sense of self-esteem sees you through. For you, success enters right through the rough and tough pathways of life.

■ ■ ■

My Learning Experience

The moment a child is born, he starts learning things about life and living. He learns to cry, laugh and attract attention. Before long, he learns from experience that a cry from his lips makes mummy come running to him. Now, whenever he wants something, he just howls and gets the desired thing or the desired result. This is the beginning of his learning profile.

Learning comes through experience. We learn from our interaction with others. Different people employ different modes of learning. Some tend to learn through their reflective observation, while others use an active experimentation approach.

These different approaches used in learning reflect different categories of persons having their characteristic learning profiles. Check which category you belong to...

Group A: Present-oriented

1. You find yourself responding to your instincts immediately – you're instinctive.

2. You feel for other's emotions and give them equal importance – you're emotional.

3. You learn from your experiences by not repeating the same mistake twice – you're experience-oriented.

4. When it comes to practical views on life, you are a hardcore realist – you're realistic.

Group B: Past-oriented

1. You are sensitive towards ways of life – you're sensitive.
2. You do not hide your feelings under false demeanour – you're reflective.
3. You are the same from inside as you reflect from the outside – you're transparent.
4. You have a sharp eye and a keen sense of observation – you're very observant.

Group C: Future-oriented

1. You have the ability to analyse a situation – you're analytical.
2. You are intelligent and possess logical skills – you're intellectual.
3. Your rational approach towards life is your best weapon – you're evaluative.
4. You have clear conceptions about everything – you're a conceptualiser.

Group D: Application-oriented

1. You love to experiment – you're experimental.
2. You have a curious and active mind – you're responsive.
3. To achieve your goal you do not mind taking risks – you're adventurous.
4. You put your knowledge to optimum use – you're enterprising.

Scoring Key

Each group has four characteristics that define the distinctive learning profile of that particular group. The characteristic that expresses your learning profile most may be given 2 marks.

You may assign 1 mark to each characteristic that least expresses you in each category.

The characteristic that does not fit in your learning profile at all will be 0.

Add up the scores assigned to each characteristic for each category separately. The category that gets the highest score is your predominant category, depicting your approach towards learning and revealing your learning profile.

Category	Score	Approach	Learning Profile
A	4–8	Practical and concrete experience	You are practical in your personal and professional life. You prefer to live in the present, taking life as it comes. You make full use of your concrete experience and believe in realism. Your friends are many and your interaction with them is warm and receptive.
B	4–8	Keen observer	Your sensitive observation and perceptive understanding are key to your balanced behavi-our. You are a keen observer and this helps you in acquiring new information and concepts. Such observational learning in various situations plays an important role in shaping your best behaviour. You look up to role models who are crucial in shaping your learning profile.
C	4–8	Analytical and logic-oriented	Your approach to learning is rational. You can categorise and evaluate any situation on logical grounds. You are an abstract conceptualiser. Your practical approach towards life is a boon in itself.

Category	Score	Approach	Learning Profile
D	4–8	Active and curious	You believe in the practical aspects of life. You turn to active experimentation. Your learning approach is based on practice, experiment and application. You have an active and curious mind that is always keen to learn and experiment. Active testing, experimenting and risk-taking give a boost to your learning profile.

■ ■ ■

My Emotional Aptitude

Emotional aptitude is determined by our ability to cope with emotional factors like anxiety, worry, resentment, boredom, feelings of non-appreciation and futility. Emotional upheavals tend to make us mentally as well as physically weak, leaving us susceptible to illness and debility, thus reducing our working capacity.

To discover your emotional aptitude, you must know the three main factors that need to be controlled: worry, tension and emotional upheavals.

So check these statements, introspect a while and truthfully answer them:

1. In a conscious effort to relax, you would join a:
   a. Meditation class.
   b. Gym.
   c. Both.

2. You came from a small town to a big metro. Most of your colleagues and roommates belong to the city itself, you:
   a. Are in awe of them.
   b. Detest them.
   c. Behave normally with everyone.

3. There is tough competition at the workplace. You need to work very hard for a promotion. Would you:
   a. Start hating your colleagues.
   b. Take undue advantage of them in a subtle manner.
   c. Do your work sincerely.

4. With nothing going right for you, you find all shades of grey surrounding you. Would you:
   a. Feel lost in them.
   b. Look for a silver lining.
   c. Give yourself a pep talk to make all the greys vanish.

5. You realise very well that you could not become what you wanted to be in life. Do you:
   a. Brood over it day and night and feel miserable.
   b. Sigh and resign yourself to fate.
   c. Synchronise dreams and reality in your favour.

6. 'Our destiny is what we make it' — do you believe in this statement:
   a. No.
   b. May be but it is not true for me.
   c. Yes.

7. Unjust criticism of your abilities evokes:
   a. Anger.
   b. Frustration.
   c. A smile, since you consider it a disguised compliment and recognition of your talents.

8. You are tired after a long day at office. You like to unwind:
   a. In front of the television.
   b. By writing a diary.
   c. By listening to soothing music.

9. In the hustle and bustle of a hectic life, this brings a smile to your lips:
   a. A fat pay packet.
   b. A day off from work.
   c. A refreshing memory of the excellent time spent with your family.

10. You are a housewife. Apart from the usual household responsibilities, your working sister-in-law has left her two small children in your care, as she has to attend a seminar for 15 days. Do you:

    a. Fret and fume and make an issue of it.
    b. Hand over the children to your mother-in-law.
    c. Remind yourself that she is also a part of your family and try to do your best.

Scoring Key

Count all the a's and assign them 3 marks each. Count all the b's and assign them 2 marks each. Count all the c's and assign them 1 mark each.

Interpretation

Score	Emotional Aptitude	Analysis
10–16	Sound emotional aptitude	You have the emotional aptitude required to make your life exciting and enjoyable. You also have the ability to shape your thoughts and emotions to best advantage. You have a pleasing personality. You are adept at avoiding unnecessary tension and energise your mind through mental relaxation techniques. You are mentally and emotionally enriched, having a sound philosophy of life. Life has a lot to offer you and you deserve it.
17–22	Fair equilibrium	You experience a fair equilibrium between mental tension and relaxation. You can deal with life's tensions through a healthy attitude. You have uncovered your hidden mental and emotional strengths, but are yet to tap them fully. You are on the right track. Keep going.

Score	Emotional Aptitude	Analysis
23–30	Emotional upheavals	You are a victim of boredom, frustration and fatigue. You are far from achieving a sense of harmony. Your approach to life is somewhat restrained and unrealistic. You start the work happily but soon get bored or fatigued because you do not find it motivating enough anymore. If only you could realise that this boredom is not caused by excess work but due to worry, frustration and resentment, your life would be much better. You need to control your emotions, so that you can approach life differently. Once you learn to handle your emotional upheavals, you will lead an enjoyable life.

■ ■ ■

Nagging Anxieties

Life is so tough these days that just living a full life is very tiring and demanding and happens to be a full-time job. The daily hassles of life prove more stressful than major, unpleasant events of life. Feelings of anxiety, fear and tension overpower all of us at some time or the other. Pleasant events in our lives have a positive effect on us and uplift our spirit.

Nagging anxieties can produce life-long harmful effects, which may turn into an anxiety disorder. We must ensure we are not prone to anxiety.

Let's check our level of anxiety by answering the following questions:

Group A

1. Criticism:
    a. Upsets you.
    b. Makes you more determined.

2. Worry:
    a. Makes you lose sleep.
    b. Gives you reason to perform better.

3. A difficult situation:
    a. Makes you nervous.
    b. Builds up your confidence.

4. An ailment:
    a. Piles up the workload.
    b. Gives you time to relax.

5. An awkward social mistake:
   a. Leaves you embarrassed for a long time.
   b. Helps you learn from the past.
6. Life is a:
   a. Burden and strain.
   b. Gift from God.
7. In a group, you feel:
   a. Lonely, bored, and tired.
   b. Great, electrified, and recharged.
8. This world and human existence is:
   a. Meaningless.
   b. Meaningful.
9. While going on an outdoor trip, do you go back to:
   a. Check the lock of the front door repeatedly.
   b. Check the main door lock once and leave.
10. A fast-paced car gives you:
    a. The jitters.
    b. A thrill.

Group B

Here are a few situations. Just tick whether you have, in the recent past, faced them with anxiety or coolly.

No.	Situation that makes you	Anxious	Cool
1.	Owing money		
2.	Short on money		
3.	Health problems		
4.	Death in the family		
5.	Trouble with neighbours		
6.	Trouble at workplace		
7.	Losing your job		
8.	Misplacing house keys		
9.	Losing money in share market		
10.	Overworked		

Scoring Key

Group A: Give 1 mark for each 'b' answer. Group B: Give 1 mark for each 'Cool' answer. Add up all the marks and check out your final score.

Interpretation

Score for Both Groups	Analysis	Corrective Measures
0–10	You are the anxious type. You tend to lose confidence and clarity of thought because of stress and anxiety. You are so involved in the situation that you get tensed up. This makes it difficult for you to view different situations with a detached perspective.	You must spend more time doing the things you enjoy. A relaxed attitude towards life will help you attain inner peace and tranquillity.
11–20	Life's little pleasures are more precious to you. They serve as a buffer between you and anxiety. Economy and stress management take you towards success. You are a favourite of everyone. You organise things better. Peace and wisdom endear you to your loved ones. You have the spontaneity and freshness of a flower. A sense of freedom leads you to greater heights and opens new horizons.	Exercise, relaxation and a healthy attitude towards life's problems will rejuvenate your health and energy levels. Your skill in the art of living is enviable. Keep it up.

■ ■ ■

God is My Guru

A French psychiatrist once said, "There is another element present in the mind beyond the conscious and the subconscious." This he termed, 'The Super Conscious'. Each human being is a powerhouse of efficient and unrealised spiritual powers. The only way of releasing these powers is by becoming an expert in the mechanism of faith.

The law of psychokinetics states that the human mind has the power to control adverse conditions, circumstances and material things when the driving energy of faith is released. It may sound queer but we all can generate more energy than a dynamo merely by means of faith and prayer. This energy is the power and strength bestowed upon us by Him for believing in Him. The key to it is to learn to have faith. Faith establishes a channel between you and Him, through which divine powers flow.

Have you ever experienced the power of spiritual touch?

Given below are a few statements. Check the ones you honestly believe in:

1. God is a:
    a. Power that runs this universe.
    b. Mystery.
    c. Myth created by religious leaders for their own benefit.
2. Do you believe:
    a. God is always with you.
    b. God is a non-entity.
    c. Seeing is believing.

3. Do you often:
   a. Set aside a few minutes and pray to God.
   b. Try to pray but faith eludes you.
   c. Wonder why people pray to somebody they can't even see.

4. When you talk to God while praying, you feel:
   a. Exhilarated.
   b. Nothing – just do it as a routine.
   c. Silly – will never do it again.

5. Events and happenings in your life are:
   a. God's will.
   b. Your efforts and God's will.
   c. Your efforts alone.

6. Do you believe that your prayers will be answered:
   a. I do.
   b. May be.
   c. No way.

7. Physical or mental illness, poverty and the troubled world remind you:
   a. About the power of God.
   b. Never to sin.
   c. To abolish the root cause of the problem.

8. The phenomenon of life after death:
   a. Affirms your faith in God's powers.
   b. Confuses you.
   c. Is not acceptable to you.

9. When you pray, you:
   a. Think positive, with total concentration.
   b. Think negative, mindful about the day's tensions.
   c. Just shut your eyes for the sake of others.

10. Destiny is:
    a. God's wish.
    b. Luck.
    c. Karma.

Scoring Key

Assign 2 marks for every 'a' answer and 1 mark for every 'b' answer.

Interpretation

Score	Trait	Analysis
0–4	Non-believer	You are unaware of what you are missing in life. You are yet to discover the power of prayer. If you pray sincerely, you will soon notice a new strength and joy. Talk to God as a friend and He will respond.
5–12	Believer	You believe in Him. You pray to Him. You have a fair insight into the divine force. You secure His guidance in all your activities. You feel the invisible power at times, which directs you in your activities and contacts. You live a God-centred life for your own satisfaction. Try praying selflessly and you will find a link developing with Him. Soon you will be showered with His blessings.
13–20	Divine faith	You are wise and fortunate enough to have this kind of faith in His powers. You draw inspiration from Him by your selfless prayers. This radiation of love and goodwill spreads all around you like an aura. Such close proximity to God gives you inner strength. No matter how much pain, difficulty, hardships and tragedy you face, you can rise above them magnificently with His love and support on your side.

■ ■ ■

The Joy of Living

There are two ways of living your life. One is while 'brimming with life' and the other is in a 'lifeless manner'. Life is in the living i.e., living life to its fullest. It is the only way in which we can appreciate this gift of God – our precious life. A discriminative attitude and perennially complaining manner takes the joy out of life, making it dull, boring and hard to endure. We can derive so much fun out of the small joys offered by life that all we have to do is notice these passing moments and turn them into our memorable, precious memories.

To some of us it comes naturally and spontaneously. Waiting for the big events in life to grant us happiness may result in a long frustrating wait. So just celebrate life's unique moments as and when you encounter them and ENJOY!

Take this quiz and find your level of happiness and joy of living:

No.	Way of Living	Yes	No
	Do you:		
1.	Enjoy fun trips and outings.		
2.	Find yourself humming often.		
3.	Sometimes gift lovely flowers to your loved ones without an occasion.		
4.	Laugh often and make others laugh too.		
5.	Live life one moment at a time.		

No.	Way of Living	Yes	No
6.	Treat yourself to your favourite things from time to time.		
7.	Plan occasions like birthdays and anniversaries and treat them with your special touch.		
8.	Often celebrate without any occasion.		
9.	Enjoy nature. It gives you a high when you get wet in the first showers of the monsoon/the first spring blossoms/ experience a nip in the air.		
10.	Fun trips and outings being your favourite, apart from going out in your free time, you also spare some time to pursue your hobbies.		

Scoring Key

Give 1 mark for all 'Yes' answers. Add your score.

Interpretation

Score	Way of living	Analysis	Measures
Less than 4	Dull life	You lead quite a dull life. Work, eat and sleep is your motto. You tend to fret about the future and crib about the present. Everything seems to fall into a rut, as you make no efforts to take those significant little breaks from daily routine.	Try putting some colour in your life by going out and meeting people. Soon you will find this world a beautiful place.

Score	Way of living	Analysis	Measures
Between 4–7	Average life	You are living life as it comes. You enjoy the fun moments in life as and when you encounter them. On your own, you make no efforts to bring these moments back repeatedly. But chances are, somewhere along the line, you may start taking life a bit too seriously and forget about the small pleasures of life, so important for your existence.	Spare some more time and discover the rich treasure of small joys to live your present moments fully.
More than 7	Enjoyable life	You are living life in the true sense. You take life in your stride with a cheerful note. You have the knack of deriving great happiness and fun from little things in life. You are capable of celebrating every moment of life. You can turn the smallest happening into a big event and celebrate it with vigour. Life is never mundane or boring for you and people around you. Your positive attitude towards life gifts you with an inimitable persona that is infectious.	You live a happy life and spread happiness around you. You are perfect in the art of enjoying life.

■ ■ ■

Weaving Dreams

Dreams are a part of our growing years. Different individuals dream of different things. Our fascinations, in-born tendencies and goals together form our dream world. Some simply keep dreaming; others turn these dreams into reality.

Dreams exhibit our approach towards life. Let's check out your approach while you weave those lovely dreams.

No.	Your dreams	Never	Sometimes	Always
1.	Do you dream of the future?			
2.	Do you visualise the past as a dream not come true?			
3.	You use your dreams to help reaffirm and realise your goals.			
4.	Dreams help you find new creative ways to solve problems in different situations.			
5.	Your loved ones share your dreams.			
6.	Your dreams are so farfetched that the outcome depresses you.			

No.	Your dreams	Never	Sometimes	Always
7.	When your dreams are not realised, do you blame yourself?			
8.	Your biggest dream is to live a creative, peaceful and happy life.			
9.	You begin with your dreams but end up realising others' dreams.			
10.	You think dreams can be turned into reality if one works towards them sincerely.			

Scoring Key

Assign marks in the following pattern:

Never: 0. Sometimes: 1. Always: 2.

But for 2, 6, 7 and 9, reverse the order of marking:

Never: 2. Sometimes: 1. Always: 0.

Interpretation

Score	Analysis	Personality
0–6	You dream, but do not wait for them to be realised. You take life as it comes. You do not like the lost feeling that comes naturally when the dreams are not realised.	Realist
7–12	You are caring, soft-hearted and live in your dream world. You prefer to live with your dreams even if they are not realised. An unrealised dream may leave you depressed, but your sensitive nature helps you overcome it. Soon you may be weaving another dream.	Dreamer
13–20	You are a dreamer who makes sure a dream is realised. You like to dream not for the heck of it, but to fulfil your dream. Your thoughtful approach, analytical power and down-to-earth manner help you achieve all that you have dreamt of in life.	Achiever

■ ■ ■

I'm a Romantic

Amidst mist, frothy springs,
holding hands you and I,
walk the hilly path,
climbing up towards those swarming clouds,
which touch our face like soft cotton balls.
We share our laughter, our sorrows,
our words and the silence too.

—A dream for a romantic

Despite the pressures of modern life, some of us work towards keeping our emotional and romantic dreams alive and hold them precious. At the same time, there are others who prefer to keep such dreams at bay.

Let's check out which category you belong to. Please tick the statements you agree with:

No.	Statements	Score
A.	I love:	
	Watching sentimental movies while holding his hand.	
	Dancing in his arms to the beat of soft romantic music.	
	Reading poems along with my partner.	
	To hear the silence of natural surroundings.	
	A walk in the moonlight.	
	The cooing of a baby.	

No.	Statements	Score
	His husky voice.	
	His caring attitude.	
	His thoughtful gestures.	
	An evening out together, leaving the kids at home.	
B.	I am fascinated by:	
	Floating clouds on a foggy evening.	
	The misty gardens smelling of freshly wet earth.	
	Morning dew sitting pretty on the petals of lovely flowers.	
	Meandering hills with tall majestic trees.	
	Blue sea waves touching my feet.	
	Mild scents evoking beautiful memories.	
	The tranquillity of a lonely path.	
	The beauty of frothy springs and dreamy waterfalls.	
	Leafless flowering trees.	
	The sight of a rainbow in a clear blue sky.	
C.	I prefer:	
	An outing with my spouse, instead of the whole family.	
	An exciting day at work rather than a walk down the street.	
	A quiet candlelight dinner for two, rather than a party with close friends.	
	Soft music with close dancing, rather than visiting a disco.	

No.	Statements	Score
	Holding his hand than holding his pay packet.	
	Cooking special dishes for him, rather than ordering the dishes from the best restaurant.	
	Watching TV after a hectic day, rather than listening to his problems at work.	
	Wearing an old sari of his choice, rather than a new jazzy outfit he abhors.	
	Visiting his family every weekend, rather than visiting my own folks.	
	To forget petty issues, rather than make a mountain out of a molehill.	

Scoring Key

Add your score for the statements you agree with.

Interpretation

Score	Analysis	Personality
0–12	You have romance on your mind but your priorities are different. You have an eye for the good things in life. You enjoy life to the fullest, surrounded by your loved ones. You love your spouse but at times just the two of you gets too lonely for you. You need company to pep up your romance.	Romance in the air
13–30	You are a romantic in the true sense. Deeply sensitive and soft-hearted, you seem to revel in highly charged relationships. You are caring about the intimate feelings of your spouse. You draw a mystic aura around yourself that makes you irresistible. You love to escape from everyday routine into your dream world.	True romantic

■ ■ ■

My Words Reveal My Inner Self

> Language springs out of the innermost parts of us. No mirror renders a man's likeness so true as his speech.
>
> —Dr Samuel Johnson

Doctor Samuel Johnson wrote these words more than three centuries ago and they still hold true today. We mould our thoughts into words and these are then used in communication. These words provide vital information about a person's psyche and inner thoughts. Oft-repeated words in a conversation are the surest clues to a person's real personality.

Review your choice of words in a conversation and discover various aspects of your personality:

1. You begin a conversation with:
   a. A cough/sniffle or throat clearing.
   b. Greeting the person.

2. You find it easy to begin a conversation with:
   a. A stranger.
   b. Someone known to you.

3. At a social gathering you are:
   a. At a loss for words.
   b. The centre of conversation.

4. When angry, you:
   a. Just stare at the person and turn back.
   b. Firmly tell the person his/her fault.
5. If someone paid you a compliment, you:
   a. Simply blush and walk away.
   b. Take it in your stride and accept it gracefully.
6. In a cinema hall, a group of girls are talking too loudly and disturbing everyone. You:
   a. Wait for someone else to tell them off.
   b. Tell them to shut up.
7. You compliment and praise your friends and close ones:
   a. After gathering much courage.
   b. Spontaneously.
8. In group activity, you are generally a:
   a. Listener.
   b. Speaker.
9. To get the work done by your subordinates, you prefer to:
   a. Send them memos.
   b. Tell them personally.
10. When you are upset with someone, you prefer to:
    a. Bottle up your resentful feelings for fear of creating an unpleasant scene.
    b. Clear the air as soon as possible.

Scoring Key

Give a minus for each 'a' answer. Give a plus for each 'b' answer. Add up all your pluses and minuses.

Interpretation

More Minuses: You are at a loss for words most of the time. It may be your natural shyness, introverted nature or an effort to keep away from controversies. But you seem to lack the quality of self-assertion. You are so soft-natured and kind that you tend to feel guilty about anything that goes wrong, whether it's your fault or not.

More Pluses: You have a way with words. Your philosophy: 'Words speak louder than action.' You live life on your own terms and dictate them too. You respect your identity and know very well how to maintain it with dignity.

■ ■ ■

My Drawbacks and Guilt Quotient

No one is flawless. Every human being has his own drawbacks and weaknesses. These drawbacks affect our functioning, thereby giving us a guilty feeling for not having completed our tasks properly. These pent-up and unrelieved guilt feelings bear a direct relationship with our behaviour patterns and problems. To manage our guilty conscience adequately, we must first try to rectify our drawbacks. Talking about our guilty feelings and drawbacks without reservations helps in relieving them, since guilt tends to fester in secrecy.

Here are a few indicators of our drawbacks and guilt-related complexes. Find out if you are prone to such feelings and then solve the problem. Please tick the questions you agree with:

No.	Statement	Yes	No
1.	When you do something right, do you give yourself credit?		
2.	As a child you were a prankster. Do you often keep recalling your actions with regret?		
3.	Do you believe: 'I am the most responsible person around. If anything goes wrong, I am responsible.'		

No.	Statement	Yes	No
4.	To make your son behave, you have always been very strict with him. Now he is in the boarding school. Do memories about him revive thoughts about your heartless behaviour towards him in his formative years?		
5.	Do others often manipulate you, which you only realise and repent about on retrospection?		
6.	You feel the perfection expected of you is far-fetched and will never come true.		
7.	Do you usually count your blessings and thank God for what you have?		
8.	Do you treat your previous mistakes as important milestones from which you can learn caution, thereby amending and directing your future life?		
9.	Someone very close to you expired while you were away for a seminar in another city. You had known of the illness but did not expect it to be life-threatening. This tragic news has riddled you with guilt. Would you let this guilty feeling overwhelm your life?		
10.	'Your promotion is someone else's demotion.' Do you believe in this dictum and often feel guilty that your success causes others to fail?		

Scoring Key

Assign 1 mark for each question you agree with, except question numbers 1, 7, and 8. For these questions, give 1 mark if you disagree with them.

Interpretation

Score	Analysis	Guilt Quotient
0–5	You suffer from true guilt. You are aware of your faults. You feel guilty and promise yourself never to repeat the mistake(s). This healthy and well-rounded attitude pays you with healthier and improved productivity. It also frees your mind of the repressed guilt factor. Discovering drawbacks and feeling guilty is a natural phenomenon, but sticking to it for a longer time than required is harmful – you are well aware of this fact.	True guilt syndrome
6–10	You are aware of your drawbacks and suffer from a severe guilty conscience. Although deep down you know that these drawbacks are not deliberate, your conscience does not allow you to accept this fact. Since you can amend the drawbacks now, this guilty feeling weakens and damages you mentally. Try and pick up the threads of your life and start afresh. Let bygones be bygones. Take hold of your life and begin it with a promise of using your previous mistakes as a lesson for the future.	False guilt syndrome

■ ■ ■

My Charm, Poise and Grace

A woman is an epitome of charm, poise and grace. She exudes these qualities through her actions. Her synchronised body movements, mannerisms to match her natural grace and a natural beauty devoid of artificial means project a confident persona. She is ready to face the world armed with her grace and elegance. Are you such a woman?

Charm, poise and grace are not easy to develop. They are, in fact, the direct manifestation of a cool mind. If a woman is at ease with herself, grace and poise come to her naturally. An obsession with acquiring these qualities only backfires, because charm, poise and grace are not available off the shelf. These are natural covert traits that only surface in congenial surroundings.

Let's take this quiz and find out how charming your mannerisms are:

1. When you step out of your room:
    a. You look naturally fresh and elegant.
    b. You look made up like a doll.

2. Your normal way of walking is:
    a. Well balanced with graceful steps.
    b. Like an athlete with hurried steps.

3. You sit with:
    a. An erect, upright posture.
    b. A slumping caved-in chest and protruding belly.

4. A graceful natural walk may be defined as:
   a. A swan floating in a lake.
   b. Straight steps with hands dangling from the side.
5. While sitting idle at home/office do you often:
   a. Do toe-moving exercises to relax.
   b. Put your feet up on the table to relax.
6. While talking to people do you unintentionally keep:
   a. Your gaze straight with a smile on your lips.
   b. Picking your nose/smoothing your hair/avoiding eye contact.
7. At social gatherings do people find you:
   a. Circulating with a drink or juice in hand.
   b. Sitting in a corner with a plate full of snacks and a drink.
8. You are aware that wherever you go:
   a. Many heads turn to look at you.
   b. Many heads turn away from you.
9. In an argument do you often:
   a. Speak in a low, modulated, firm voice.
   b. Shout louder than the other person.
10. You prefer to:
    a. Act and behave naturally.
    b. Ape your favourite cine star's mannerism.

Scoring Key

Give yourself 5 marks for every 'a' and 2 marks for every 'b'.

Interpretation

Score	Analysis
0–25	It's true that style, charm, grace and poise cannot be imitated but you can come close to these traits by not being too loud in your action, adjusting your posture and body language suitably and by bringing an element of maturity in the manner you deal with others. Try this and you will find a vast difference in the attitude of others towards you.
26–50	Your charm, grace and poise are a matter of envy. You have the style that comes to you naturally. Others envy you for your natural style that cannot be imitated. You are a jewel in the crown. Keep glowing.

■ ■ ■

My Strengths, My Relationships

The bond we share with our loved ones gives us inner strength to deal with the calamities of life. During the course of living, we form many relationships, ranging from close and loving, practical and work-oriented to intimate and romantic ones. There may be times when we feel lonely despite being surrounded by people. Essentially, loneliness reflects the absence of satisfying relationships.

Let's find out how satisfying our relationships are and whether they make us feel lonely or give us a sense of emotional security.

Quiz A

1. Coming from a nuclear family, you are married into a joint family. Do you:
   a. Feel suffocated.
   b. Enjoy the company.

2. Your mother-in-law is against your going out to work. Would you:
   a. Obey her but seethe inwardly.
   b. Try to make her understand your point of view.

3. Your husband received a promotion. He has brought two tickets for a movie tonight. You are happy for him but tomorrow is your son's class test. Would you:
   a. Refuse to go and ask him to take his friend instead.

b. Leave your son with his grandparents and tell him that you'll help him the moment you come back. Till then he can learn on his own.
4. You believe in the principle of:
   a. Everything has its price; if you pay, you get it.
   b. All relationships are based on trust.
5. The crab mentality of pulling others down for your own benefit:
   a. Is today's practical truth.
   b. Damages human relationships.

Quiz B

Tick 'Yes' or 'No' for these statements.

No.	Statement	Yes	No
	Do you often:		
1.	Feel the need for emotional security.		
2.	Look for an intimate individual whom you could turn to.		
3.	Find yourself drifting away from your near and dear ones.		
4.	Feel left out in a group.		
5.	Feel you have a lot in common with others.		
6.	Feel your relationships are rather superficial.		
7.	Relate to your people easily.		
8.	Find others more caring and loving than yourself.		
9.	Feel that people are around you but not with you.		
10.	Feel that your overreaction to issues is distancing you from people.		

Scoring Key

In Quiz A, for all 'b' answers assign 1 mark each.
In Quiz B, for statements 5, 7 and 8 assign 1 mark for each 'Yes' answer.
For all other statements, assign 1 mark for each 'No'.

Interpretation

Score	Relationship	Analysis
0–8	Weak relationships	You are vulnerable to loneliness because you are unable to build strong emotional ties in a relationship. Perhaps your belief of your own unworthiness limits your growing relationships with others. You tend to blame weak ties on others rather than your own personal inadequacies. Focus on building up strong relationships with your near and dear ones. Develop your interpersonal skills, and open your arms to have access to a network of social ties, close friends and relatives and experience the charm of healthy relationships.
8–15	Strong relationships	You are a well-adjusted, emotionally sensitive individual with satisfying emotional and social relationships. You value your relationships above all. At times when you are at the crossroad of a relationship, you take the rational approach and emerge a winner. In a relationship you tend to give as much as you receive. Your relationships are your strength in the true sense.

■ ■ ■

The Desire to Prove Myself

At home, you are the centre of all activities. You take decisions and others follow them without murmur. At work, you are always on the go, looking for new goals and meeting your targets. Your self-motivation is the reason for doing worthwhile things. This motivation comes from the desire to prove yourself to one and all.

But if you find yourself making excuses and not being able to deliver results, the chances are you lack the desire to prove yourself. You suffer from lack of motivation and a desire to prove yourself.

Let's take the following quiz and check how strong your motivation level is. Tick 'Yes' or 'No' for these statements.

No.	Statement	Yes	No
	Do you often feel:		
1.	Although you are very busy, you are not getting appropriate results.		
2.	There is too much work but too little time.		
3.	Life is so monotonous with all work and no play.		
4.	That your growth is stunted, so you feel stagnated.		
5.	A sense of imbalance at work and home.		

No.	Statement	Yes	No
6.	That you need to improve your decision-making abilities.		
7.	Neither peaceful nor excited about the life.		
8.	Other people pose problems by making it difficult to turn your resolutions into reality.		
9.	Creative and spontaneous.		
10.	Autonomous, by remaining true to yourself despite pressure to change.		

Scoring Key

For every 'Yes' answer give yourself 1 mark, except for answers 3, 4, 5, 7 and 8. For these, give 1 mark for each 'No' answer.

Interpretation

Score	Analysis	Type
0–3	You certainly need motivation to be an achiever in life. But you must remember motivation cannot be borrowed from others. It has to be cultivated. One important way to do this is by setting your aims and acting in alignment with them. You can set role-related goals for improvement. Introspect and set realistic goals for yourself.	Need motivation
4–6	You are a self-confident person and sufficiently motivated. You are familiar with the basic rule in life, i.e., doing the most important things first. You choose moderately difficult but realistic tasks to attain success in your work. Your goal-centred living carves out a life of happiness, fulfilment and tremendous results for you.	Self-confident achiever

Score	Analysis	Type
7–10	The desire to prove yourself and take up the challenges of life is strong in you. You successfully use your self-awareness, conscience, independent will and creative imagination to fulfil your dreams and achieve your goals. You are highly motivated and show a preference for challenging tasks and follow the pursuit of excellence. You are agile, vibrant and desire to perform to the best of your ability. You believe in reaching the top through healthy competition. Your desire to prove yourself inculcates leadership qualities in you.	Empowered personality

■ ■ ■

My Fears and Phobias

The only thing we have to fear is fear itself.
—Roosevelt

Fear is a realistic response by us towards any perceived danger. It is also a natural phenomenon. It generates the fight response in our bodies and gives us the strength to tackle a situation.

When fear persists over a great length of time and intensifies, it becomes a phobia. Phobias rob us of our mental as well as physical health.

Answer these questions truthfully and discover your hidden fears and phobias.

No.	Phobia	Yes	No
1.	While at meetings or outings or while giving lectures, do you feel everyone is staring at you?		
2.	Do you repeatedly lock doors, arrange things, wash hands, wash clothes and utensils?		
3.	Do you often suffer from palpitations despite getting a clear ECG (electro-cardiogram) report?		
4.	Stepping out in the dark or entering a lonely house brings persistent, senseless thoughts and impulses accompanied by strange images.		

No.	Phobia	Yes	No
5.	Two months ago you were a witness to a crime. You have not been able to remove the incident from your mind till now. You still dream about it and wake up sweating profusely.		

No.	Fears	Yes	No
	I fear:		
1.	My exams, due to which I always get nervous and fail to perform efficiently.		
2.	The deadlines in my office that I feel I can never meet.		
3.	The financial ups and downs because I know I can never overcome them.		
4.	Watching a horror film, as it will haunt me at night.		
5.	A cockroach/lizard/rat, even though I know they are harmless.		

Scoring Key

Assign 2 marks for every 'Yes' answer and assign 1 mark for every 'No' answer. Add the score.

Interpretation

Score	Analysis	Measures
10–15	Fears and phobias are a part of life but you are lucky to have the ability to confront and change your fear-causing beliefs into positive ones. You experience fear but do not remain in its clutches for more than a brief period of time. You are capable of acting appropriately.	You are strong enough to overcome your fear and phobias. You may further boost your energy levels thro-ugh meditation.

Score	Analysis	Measures
16–20	Your fears are unreasonable and too long-drawn for the concerned event. Some of them may have turned into phobias. You have now learned to live with them, which is your biggest mistake. Initially, a fear may be gripping but if you do not shake it off then and there but allow it to sink in, it tends to grow on you and turn into a phobia.	You are aware of your fears and phobias. That is the first step in curing them. Remind yourself often that these fears are imaginary. Keep your mind occupied in fruitful activities.

■ ■ ■

Perfection Personified

> As I mounted up the hill
> The music in my heart I bore
> Long after it was heard no more.
> —William Wordsworth

A woman plays varied roles in life. She is the obedient daughter, loving wife, dutiful daughter-in-law and an affectionate mother – all rolled into one. Above all, she is a woman. This is a role she portrays for her own self-esteem and satisfaction.

Do you think you portray all these qualities to perfection? Take this quiz and find out.

The Perfect Daughter

1. Your best friend is your:
    a. Classmate.
    b. Sister.
    c. Mother.
2. At times, you have a difference of opinion with your mother. Such arguments always end with you:
    a. Staging a walkout.
    b. Bursting into tears.
    c. Apologising to your mother.
3. You bring your boyfriend home because you want him to:
    a. Recognise your financial status.
    b. Meet your father.
    c. Meet your mother.

4. You aspire to be like your mother because:
   a. You are her daughter.
   b. Every woman faces the same destiny.
   c. She is your role model.
5. Your mother has recovered from a long illness. You:
   a. Feel relieved because you can now go out with friends.
   b. Feel inadequate, thinking you wasted all that time.
   c. Beam with joy at the thought of having your loving mother around you soon.

The Perfect Wife

1. You had planned to go out for dinner but your husband returns from work and tells you he is very tired and in no mood to go out. Do you:
   a. Seethe inwardly but outwardly express sympathy.
   b. Seethe openly, showing your resentment clearly.
   c. Make arrangements at home, empathising with him.
2. Regardless of how long you have been married, how often do you prepare your husband's favourite dishes solely to please him:
   a. Sometimes.
   b. Hardly ever.
   c. Regularly.
3. When your husband talks to you, do you:
   a. Listen to him absentmindedly.
   b. Never pay attention.
   c. Listen to him intently.
4. Can you honestly admit that during your married life, you have never tried to change your husband's thinking and style of living and:
   a. Gave up trying long ago.
   b. Are still trying.
   c. Never tried.

5. How long ago did you cease dressing up and making up to please and attract only your husband:
   a. Fairly recently.
   b. Cannot remember.
   c. Haven't ceased doing these things.

Special Question

Get your hubby to answer this one for you:

Does he think of you as a:
a. Real helpmate.
b. Jolly good partner.
c. Soul mate.

Perfect Daughter-in-law

1. When you entered your in-laws' house, you saw your mother-in-law as your:
   a. Husband's mother.
   b. Rival.
   c. Own mother.
2. Your mother-in-law is not feeling well but you have an important meeting at the office. Would you:
   a. Make arrangements for her, like keeping food and medicine near her bedside, then leave for work.
   b. Leave for office on time, since she is not a small child.
   c. Arrange for someone to be with her till you come back as soon as your meeting is over.
3. Your mother-in-law likes you to dress up in traditional dresses like a sari or suit, but you find them unsuitable for office. Would you:
   a. Try to make her understand your problem.
   b. Ignore her and wear clothes of your own choice – after all, it's your life.
   c. Wear them for a few days to please her and then tell her about your genuine problem.

4. You and your husband planned a quiet evening out when your mother-in-law informed you that your sister-in-law (her daughter) is coming over for dinner. Would you:
   a. Include them also in your plans.
   b. Let her deal with your sister-in-law – she is her daughter after all.
   c. Postpone your plans for another day.

5. In a function in the house most of the work is delegated and done by:
   a. Your mother-in-law.
   b. Other relatives.
   c. You.

The Perfect Mother

1. You have a promising career when your first child is born. But you have no one to look after the baby at home. Would you:
   a. Arrange for a maid.
   b. Send the baby to the crèche.
   c. Skip your career till the baby grows up.

2. Your daughter is having annual day celebrations in her school in which she is actively taking part. Unfortunately, it coincides with an Annual General Meeting in your office, where your presence is compulsory. Would you:
   a. Try to reason with the child.
   b. Refuse to go to her school since your meeting is more important.
   c. Send her father so that she does not feel left out.

3. Your child is down with high fever when suddenly your sister-in-law's would-be mother-in-law drops in. As a daughter-in-law, you are expected to attend to them and arrange for their lavish lunch and other things. Would you:
   a. Keep checking the child in between the work.

b. Leave the ill child unattended and rush to the kitchen.
   c. Arrange for someone to be with the child until you are free from your guests.
4. Your son is very naughty. He was climbing a metal ladder when you tried to stop him. He did not listen and fell from a height, suffering a bad fall. You:
   a. Bandage his wound, reminding him continuously that he has been punished for not listening to you.
   b. Spank him hard for not listening to you.
   c. Pick him up gently, bandage his wound and save the preaching for later.
5. Life comes full circle for you when your daughter brings her boyfriend home to meet you. Would you:
   a. Look at him suspiciously.
   b. Scold him left and right and throw him out.
   c. Invite him in like any other friend of hers.

The Perfect Woman

1. In your opinion, people say nice things about you:
   a. In front of you only.
   b. Hardly ever.
   c. Behind your back also.
2. You help people beyond your limits to:
   a. Impress people.
   b. Get your own work done.
   c. Express genuine concern.
3. You are a working woman, juggling your home and work:
   a. Somehow managing.
   b. In a terrible state.
   c. In a smooth run.
4. In an effort to prove yourself a superwoman managing all fields of life, are you actually:
   a. Overstraining yourself.
   b. Getting bored.
   c. Enjoying yourself.

5. You have a loving family, a good job, and emotional and financial security. You feel:
   a. Something is amiss.
   b. Life is too monotonous.
   c. Content with life.

Scoring Key

Give yourself 2 marks for each 'C' answer and 1 mark for each 'A' answer. Add up the score from all the five quizzes. For the Special Question in Quiz 2, the scoring key is as follows: A = 2, B = 1, C = 5. Add this separately to the score.

Interpretation

Score	Analysis
0–21	The various roles are taking their toll on you. Every role has got different expectations and responsibilities. You try to perform but somewhere along the line you lose touch. Perhaps a little more sincere effort on your part will work wonders for your life.
22–35	Everybody expects you to play the Perfect Role Model. No compromises. The perfect wife, perfect mother, perfect cook, a perfect homemaker and a perfect working woman earning a handsome salary. You find yourself juggling all these roles simultaneously. You are trying and managing pretty well except for a few misses here and there. They are permissible. Remember, no one is perfect.
36–50	You are the perfect woman. Roles roll before you in quick succession. You might have to play many of them simultaneously at a given point of time. This is what everyone expects from you. Expectations are high and the obstacles are many. But you manage perfectly well because instead of just fulfilling expectations, you relate to your people in a loving manner, making them realise your point of view as well. It is your love, care, attention and sincerity for them that have won half the battle. The rest is easy for an affectionate and dedicated perfect woman like you. Congratulations!

■ ■ ■

25 Tips for the Final Touches

> ...And miles to go before I sleep.
> —Robert Frost

This exhaustive quiz is an eye-opener tackling all aspects we have covered till now. These questions are actually your perceptions and reactions. The score is not going to put you in a certain category or declare you a particularly gifted woman. However, it will definitely boost your opinion about your own capabilities and guide you on whether you need to introspect or go in for a major personality overhaul.

It is a self-help test. Being honest with your answers is the first step towards improving your Sensitivity and Emotional Quotient. Some of these situations may not be applicable to you, but imagine what your response would have been if you were in this situation. Check it out. I am sure you will enjoy it immensely. Good luck!

1. I have known my strength and weaknesses for years. I feel:
   a. It's time for improvement.
   b. I am too old to change.
   c. I am the best.

2. When people show faith in me, I feel:
   a. Strong and competent.
   b. I am cheating them.
   c. I am too good for them.

3. If I am assigned a task, I perform my best:
   a. At all times.
   b. When no one is observing me.
   c. When someone is watching me – to impress them.

4. I am always helping people because I:
   a. Genuinely like them.
   b. Want to create a good image in their eyes.
   c. Have no choice.

5. My friends enjoy my company because I am:
   a. Fun-loving.
   b. Rich.
   c. Always pulling others' legs.

6. When someone does me a favour, I wonder:
   a. What a wonderful person s/he is.
   b. How to pay him/her back.
   c. What is his/her hidden agenda in this.

7. An emotional person makes me:
   a. Emotional too.
   b. Uncomfortable.
   c. Bored.

8. When I hear about someone's problem, I:
   a. Think of many solutions.
   b. Try to shake him off as soon as possible.
   c. Give him/her a cold shoulder.

9. I feel I am quite competent. Often, people turn to me for help. My capabilities are my:
   a. Treasure.
   b. Weakness.
   c. Troubles.

10. When I have to do something which I do not really enjoy doing but cannot avoid either, I:
    a. Do it immediately and get it over with.
    b. Postpone it till I cannot avoid it any longer.
    c. Find someone else to do it for me.

11. In my opinion, happiness is:
    a. Freedom to live life your own way.
    b. Lots of money.
    c. An illusion.

12. When I face corruption and mismanagement in real life, I:
    a. Step back and reassess the situation.
    b. Take it out on someone else.
    c. Flow with the tide.

13. When I break a rule, I:
    a. Feel bad.
    b. Forget about it soon.
    c. Give a damn.

14. When I fail to achieve something due to lack of efforts on my part, I:
    a. Rightly take the blame.
    b. Give varied reasons for the failure.
    c. Blame it on others.

15. I discuss my personal feelings and intimate details with:
    a. No one.
    b. Close friends.
    c. Everyone.

16. I prefer to praise someone through:
    a. Direct conversation.
    b. Letters and written messages.
    c. Keep it to myself, so as not to spoil that person by too much praise.

17. I make friends:
    a. Easily.
    b. Not till I know the person well.
    c. Only after a long association.

18. I feel the best time to reveal bad or shocking news to the family is when:

a. Everyone is together.
   b. Everyone is in a relaxed mood.
   c. They are already surrounded with troubles – how does one more problem matter?

19. To deal with a major problem, I:
    a. Often find myself competent enough.
    b. Seek advice and support from friends and relatives.
    c. Pretend it does not exist.

20. I do what people expect me to do even when I disagree with them:
    a. Rarely.
    b. Sometimes.
    c. Quite often.

21. If you are having a heated argument with your husband, you would:
    a. Stop awhile and let the moment pass so that you both can cool down.
    b. Instead of bottling it up, let the anger out.
    c. Just walk away.

22. Your best friend lost her job last week. She is on the lookout for a new job. Would you:
    a. Help her in every possible way.
    b. Suggest she contact job consultants.
    c. Give her a big lecture on the scarcity of jobs today.

23. After rejecting many suitors, a marriage proposal has come your way and the boy and his credentials are very good. But his family is not financially well off. Would you accept it:
    a. Because money isn't everything.
    b. Out of desperation.
    c. Because you feel you will have an upper hand since you come from a wealthier family.

24. Your result for a competition exam is out. You spent a lot of time and effort so you were expecting good

results. Unfortunately, you could not get through. Would you:
   a. Prepare for the exam again.
   b. Brood over it for some time.
   c. Never appear for a competition exam.

25. Your philosophy in life is:
    a. Set realistic goals.
    b. Set challenging goals.
    c. Not to set any goals and just float with the tide.

Scoring Key

For each 'a' answer give yourself 3 marks. For each 'b' answer give yourself 1 mark. There are no marks for any 'c' answers. Add up the score.

Interpretation

Score 0–25: You need more motivation. You are not taking full advantage of your potential. You are considered critical, inexpressive, detached, cold and a blame-shifting person. To improve your image, you will have to work on enhancing your personality and perceptions with motivation, creativity, resilience and persistence.

Score 26–50: You have a positive attitude and adapt well to the changed circumstances. Most often you can deal with stress, and interact and communicate with others effectively. But at times you become a victim of anxiety, depression, and guilt, low self-esteem and stress. Every now and then, you need motivation to come out of this state of mind.

Score 51–75: You look at life optimistically and positively. You are comfortable not only with yourself but with others also. You know and appreciate your talents and strong points, but at the same time, you are aware of your weaknesses and problem areas. You work on them and try to eliminate as many as you can.

■ ■ ■

A Woman's Guide to Personality Development

The Perfect Woman:
- ✔ Believes in honest self-analysis and starting afresh.
- ✔ Manages to overcome insecurities, complexes and doubts.
- ✔ Maintains high self-esteem.
- ✔ Has higher emotional and sensitivity levels.
- ✔ Lives life by cherished values.
- ✔ Manages stress skilfully.
- ✔ Gives importance to mental and physical fitness.
- ✔ Has a support group in the form of friends and family.
- ✔ Exudes charm, grace and poise as part of her persona.
- ✔ Is free from phobias, fears and anxieties.
- ✔ Understands the commitment level in a relationship.
- ✔ Believes in spiritual power.
- ✔ Explores new phases and challenges in life with each passing year.

Do you possess all these qualities? Yes! Congratulations! You are the PERFECT WOMAN!

■■■

Author: S.P. Sharma
Format: Paperback
Language: English
Pages: 120

Author: Prof. Shrikant Prasoon
Format: Paperback
Language: English
Pages: 200

Author: Bibhu Prasad Mishra
Format: Paperback
Language: English
Pages: 233

In a world marked by competition, personality is the key to success – whether it is social or business or personal or political arena. Interview for IAS or an MNC, meeting with the parents of your prospective bride, addressing a public rally, or delivering a speech in an international conference...if you have a confident and pleasing personality, you will surely make your mark! This book seeks to motivate young men and women, particularly students, to make conscious and continuous effort to build character and develop good personality.

Group Discussions (GD) are commonly used to assess several personality aspects of candidates during various entrance tests and as a part of selection process for various jobs. This book can be a game changer for most students, since even most technically sound and brilliant students often falter at GD.

This comprehensive guide book helps you clear the fog surrounding GD and its step-by-step instructions will make you a winner in GD.

This book includes:

• Insight into: Need of GD, Do's & Don'ts in GD, Body Language & Public Speaking, Skills & Ability required in GD, and so on

• Important GD topics, How to gather Information for GD, Reading & Practice for GD

The book 'Preparing for a Winning Interview' is divided into two sections. The first section deals with the preparations, research and understanding various facts of the interview and its procedure.

The second section contains understanding and learning specific job skills in ever-changing and challenging corporate environment; the role of an employee and the need to be prepared beforehand to fit in different organisation by meeting tough corporate tasks, and by coping with the changing works, conditions and milieu.

The book covers all the core areas of interview process, delicacies in work environment, intricacies of challenging spheres, the need of sustainbility, and presents ready and easy solutions.

visit our online bookstore: **www.vspublishers.com**

Author: Prem P Balla
Format: Paperback
Language: English
Pages: 175

Author: Navneet Mehra, Ishita Bhown
Format: Paperback
Language: English
Pages: 132

Author: Aparna Chattoupadhyay
Format: Paperback
Language: English
Pages: 176

Every man aspires to project an image of poise, positivity and personal charm. But few men really know how to achieve this. In this context, The Portrait of a Complete Man acts as an indispensable guidebook.

The book gives pointers that include: the power of perseverance and positivity; developing personal magnetism, poise and manners; cultivating healthy habits; tackling personal and sexual problems; enjoying love, marriage and fatherhood; succeeding at the workplace; handling people; improving efficiency; recognising the importance of recreation; and growing old gracefully.

The book gives practical guidelines on how a man can discover peace, happiness and contentment and become complete perfect.

The book can be very handy and useful to anyone, who wants to deliver powerful presentations. The whole book has been organized in a reader-friendly manner, giving all the desired details to help in the development of contents and delivery skills of readers.

The book has been supplemented with many case studies and examples to make it more interesting. The book comes accompanied by an interactive CD containing a PowerPoint Presentation for better understanding. The book will act as a valuable guide for all its readers to remove the barriers of effective communication.

Some of the highlights of the book are:

Finding Context to your; Presentation; Organizing It; Tailoring It; Remembering It; Rehearsing It; Delivering It

This fascinating book authored by Dr. Aparna Chattopadhyay offers you a new vision of self-awareness which would enable you to assess your feelings, capabilities and aptitudes. As you develop self-awareness, you will not only be able to identify the emotional patterns in your life and will manage them well, but will also be able to activate all-round personality development.

It will help you lead life more powerfully than before through a wide range of Psychological Quizzes.

This book enables you to:

- Generate fresh enthusiasm and ambition in your life
- Live more happily and effectively
- Build self-confidence and develop inner peace
- Enjoy better interpersonal relationships

visit our online bookstore: **www.vspublishers.com**

Author: Surendra Dogra 'Nirdosh'
Format: Paperback
Language: English
Pages: 112

Author: Vinay Mohan Sharma
Format: Paperback
Language: English
Pages: 120

Author: Seema Gupta
Format: Paperback
Language: English
Pages: 156

Have you ever thought of addressing an audience and making them listen to you without batting an eyelid? Do you want to create a trance-like spell on people listening to your speech?

It has carefully dissected every aspect of public speaking and presents a clear map that any aspiring speaker can follow. Besides, it also incorporates the necessary techniques to motivate, captivate, and persuade the audience while making various presentations, etc.

You will master 'How to'
- Conquer stage fright
- Organize material in a flowing manner
- Customise speech for different sets of gathering
- Inspire audience

Communication is not always through sound or language. Much can be said with gestures or movement of eyes. In fact, more often than not, the Body Language says more than words.

Now discover all the finer points and nuances of body language in this masterly work:
- How thumb gesture displays dominance, superiority and aggression
- How dilation of eyes sends romantic signal
- How a sideways glance indicates either hostility or interest

The book deals exhaustively with the varied nuances of etiquette and good manners for all important occasions. A handy guide for all age-groups to constantly cultivate the acumen of polished behaviour to outshine in all spheres of life.

Children are inquisitive and imitative by nature. Let their perception absorb the bonhomie, cheerfulness and courtesy all around for an overall growth of their personalities.

All the important aspects of tricky situations and how to handle them have been dealt with in detail. Posture, building relationships, communication skills – to mention just a few. Each instance merits discretion and tact.

visit our online bookstore: **www.vspublishers.com**

www.ingramcontent.com/pod-product-compliance
Lightning Source LLC
Chambersburg PA
CBHW070336230426
43663CB00011B/2333